OPEN BUSINESS SCHOOL

Information Systems Development for Managers

Richard Maddison	*The Open University*
Robert Baldock	*Arthur Andersen & Co.*
Love Bhabuta	*Palomar Research Institute*
Paul Feldman	*Arthur D. Little Ltd.*
Guy Fitzgerald	*University of Warwick*
Keith Hindle	*BIS Applied Systems*
Almos Kovacs	*MIPAC Associates; and Hatfield Polytechnic*
Aden Lane	*ICL*
Gilbert Mansell	*Huddersfield Polytechnic*
Nahed Stokes	*King's College, University of London*
Bob Wood	*Bristol Polytechnic*

Edited by Richard Maddison

Paradigm in association with The Open University

Paradigm Publishing Ltd
Avenue House, 131-133 Holland Park Avenue, London W11 4UT

The Open University
Walton Hall, Milton Keynes MK7 6AA

First published 1989

Designed by the Graphic Design Group of the Open University

Printed in Great Britain by Staples Printers Ltd, Rochester

British Library Cataloguing in Publication Data

Information systems development for managers
    1. Management. Information Systems
    I. Maddison, Richard
    658.4´038

    ISBN 0 948825 47 2

CONTENTS

PREFACE

Technological advances have made possible the development of information systems that make vast amounts and varieties of information available to many people. Various tools and techniques to aid development and implementation of such systems have become available. But as the varieties of types of information, the number of user requirements and the complexity of information systems increase, people need advice on how to plan for, coordinate and manage the developments and system changes, as well as how to plan for, develop and manage the information systems themselves.

This book provides and discusses a framework for such information systems planning, development and management. Tools and techniques such as data analysis, normalization, data dictionaries and development methodologies are not explained here: we give the overall framework into which they fit.

In preparing this book we have tried to be comprehensive and produce proposals that would be regarded as good current practice and appeal to a wide readership.

This book is intended for five types of reader:

- **information-systems policy makers,** such as *senior managers* responsible for an organization's corporate policy on information system development

- **information-systems decision makers,** including information system *middle management* and perhaps corresponding *managers in end-user departments*, who carry out the overall policy and are responsible for main information system development and maintenance decisions and recommendations

- **information-systems researchers and developers** concerned professionally with the advancement of information systems analysis and design

- **information-systems developers, designers** and **builders,** responsible for the development, implementation and maintenance of information systems and for supporting activities; including analysts, designers, programmers, data administrators and database administrators

- **information-systems teachers and students** involved in courses for any of the above types of people.

The authors formed a self-established team to research and develop the contents. Thanks are due to our organizations where they have supported their employees in participating. The views in this book are those of the individuals and not necessarily those of their organizations.

All the authors prepared internal working papers and helped draft this book. We are grateful to Leonard Capper for his comments and suggestions.

We acknowledge the help of Doreen Tucker, Christine Love, Norma Roberts and Kim Curtis of the Open University Mathematics Faculty, and Joan Williams of the Open Business School, for word processing the manuscript.

As editor I have written *we* to mean the authors, and *you* to mean the reader.

Richard Maddison
October 1988

SUMMARY

This book proposes a **framework** for the planning, development, and management of information systems (ISs). Until recently, the main concentration of the development of methods in this area has been on detailed procedures and techniques. Our proposed framework takes some emphasis away from the idea of a rigid sequence of activities.

The framework has three aspects:

- the **planning** aspect, with various levels of detail
- the **development phases** themselves
- the **review and control** function.

The *highest level of planning* within an organization is **Business Strategic Planning**. The Business Strategic Plan (BSP) clarifies the basic philosophy of the organization and states organization-wide targets. A Business Strategic Plan is not information-systems oriented, let alone computer oriented, but it will influence the planning of information systems.

Information Systems Planning includes:

- strategic planning of all ISs
- tactical planning for each IS
- project planning for each IS project.

An organization-wide **Information Systems Strategic Plan** (ISSP) then builds on the BSP in terms of the particular information systems that are required to be developed, and the priorities and plans for doing so. An 'information system' (IS) is regarded as being wider in scope than an individual computer application.

Each information system needs an **Information System Tactical Plan** (ISTP) which translates the higher-level strategic plans into plans for effective action. This may include overall planning and coordination of the later main phases such as analysis, user design, technical design and implementation. These *phases* may be in one sense sequential, but are usually and advantageously overlapped with *iterative refinement in increasing detail*, for example by prototyping. Planning the continuing future evolution of existing large information systems can be problematical, for example how to merge large existing systems.

Each project within one or more information systems needs **Information System Project Planning** (ISPP). A **project** may be one or several phases. **Project management** concerns the planning and internal review and control of the stages, tasks and activities, and with relating the individual project to the overall objectives of the organization. It involves:

- analysing the project into tasks and activities to be done
- estimating the work content
- planning, scheduling and allocating resources
- reviewing and controlling performance
- controlling change.

Actions are classified into:

- developments, which involve many phases, tasks and activities
- phases, which involve many tasks and activities
- tasks, which involve many activities
- activities.

An appropriate **management cycle** can be applied to each action, with its planning, feedback, review and control. The management cycle for any action involves:

- planning it
- doing it
- reviewing and controlling it.

The **review and control** involve extra activities both during doing the action and after doing it. These extra activities can be viewed as a review and control loop, which affects decisions, and enables prevention of more undesirable situations. Milestones are used to highlight achievements. Quality assurance and control, an essential component of review and control, can be helped by walkthroughs, inspections, quality circles and audit teams. Pitfalls and conflicts may be reduced or avoided.

Actions may be *repeated* and *interrupted* in various ways. Usually the sequencing of different actions arises because a product from one is a prerequisite for another. Generally the second action can be started as soon as a primitive version of the appropriate product is available. Prototyping, evolution, parallel development and incremental development in any combination thus fit within the framework.

The **management of planning** is itself an activity of varying scale depending on the complexity of the actions, and thus may degenerate into a trivial activity or may require meetings.

A **feasibility study** may arise *either implicitly* as part of a detailed planning step within a management cycle of some previously agreed larger action, *or explicitly* as an action in its own right. The purpose is usually to reduce uncertainty when making decisions, for example between alternatives.

The purposes of any **analysis** phase are to gain a thorough understanding of the organization's business and its information requirements, and to record systematically the information about these in a manner that assists good design decisions. As well as meeting all known and future user requirements the aims may include flexibility, maintainability and low-cost implementation and maintenance. This expands into data analysis and functional analysis. It covers existing, new and changing requirements, and knowledge of existing information systems. Generally analysis should cover a broader area than is required for the information system currently being developed, to ensure the coordination with other information systems needed for good interfaces and future flexibility. These analysis tasks should yield the appropriate design prerequisites.

Design separates into *User Design* (UD) and *Technical Design* (TD). **User Design** involves:

- deciding the best facility to support each business function
- specifying computer procedures from the end-user viewpoint
- designing non-computerized procedures, the layout of forms, reports, screens and dialogues
- estimating performance requirements
- review to check consistency with objectives
- evaluation of costs and benefits
- end-user training
- transition to each new information system or version.

This may be aided by implementing a kernel of the system and incrementally adding further levels of facilities, with feedback from end-users.

Technical Design involves iteratively defining precisely how the required system is to be constructed. This includes hardware and software configurations, database and file structures, application programs, and query languages. It also includes decisions about factors such as sizing that affect operation of the proposed system, and facilities for security, integrity, recovery, tuning, performance evaluation and feedback. The result should be a design that is technically feasible, practical to operate, easy to use, satisfactorily flexible and durable. As in all technical design, compromises are needed.

By good **project management** - including project planning and control methods - realistic dates should be estimated, agreed and achieved. Various reasons for failure and problems have been observed and ways to avoid or overcome these are suggested. Internal control of project activities should be appropriately related to each particular project and thus to the overall objectives of the organization. Many procedures familiar to professional engineers and architects can successfully be applied to information system management and control. Projects can be analysed into phases, tasks, activities, events and milestones, with estimates, work plan and resource allocation.

The summary chart overleaf gives an overview of the framework for the planning, development and management of ISs presented in the book. The terms, concepts and rationale are described in detail in later sections.

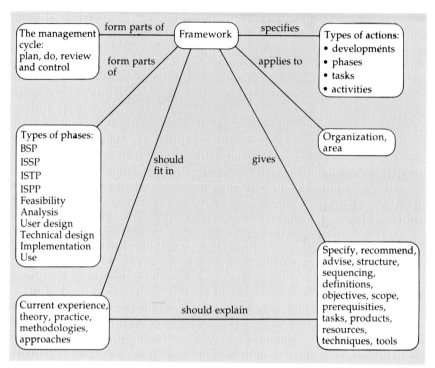

Overview of the framework for the planning, development and management of ISs.

I INTRODUCTION

1 THE BOOK

1.1 Background

We, the authors, came together partly out of an observation of the convergence of a number of methodologies for data analysis and database design, and also of non-database-oriented structured analysis and design methodologies. We decided to look more widely at the requirements for strategy, analysis and design methods in an information systems environment - incorporating up-to-date ideas and tools (e.g. databases, data dictionaries, prototyping, fourth-generation languages (4GL) and application development aids).

Our main objective was to propose a framework that could be applied to any information systems development - regardless of size, complexity, development tools and operational software. Key constraints were that the framework should cater for current and (if possible) future approaches to systems building, and should be flexible enough to remain applicable in 10 years time.

To discuss particular commercially-available methodologies was not an aim. Some of us also spent time looking at these methodologies [MADD83ISM], but for this book a more radical rethink was attempted.

The need for such a radical rethink arose from observing the dissatisfaction felt by both users and practitioners to some past approaches to systems development. This dissatisfaction, in turn, arises from a number of possible causes:

- the trends in the relative costs of hardware, software and people are increasing the importance attached to development productivity
- systems previously defined separately from each other are nowadays becoming more likely to overlap and be linked or merged and thus cause interfacing problems, as more of an organization's information processing becomes computer-based
- user expectations have changed very radically with the arrival of query languages, view data, personal microcomputers and electronic office products.

However, the task of arranging for user representatives and managers to define their information systems needs has not become any easier. The human problems remain. The methodologies of the future must somehow overcome these problems, and allow for even more user participation by even more evolutionary, incremental, prototyping approaches to systems development.

Our framework attempts to follow this course by allowing for plans to be established that allow for appropriate iteration and overlapping both within and between the development phases.

The vast variety of types of systems and applications contribute to the diversity of the many development methodologies. Producing micro-based office automation, mainframe real-time systems, computer-aided design and management information systems need different methodologies. We do *not* attempt to find a *best* methodology for the various types of systems and applications, rather we look for a *consensus* among the methodologies by defining a coherent framework covering all aspects.

Thus we aim to provide a description and checklist of what should be carried out, and how activities should fit together. We leave open the choices of techniques and tools - which evolve continually. This does not provide solutions to every problem, but may provide guidelines to facilitate better management of information system development.

The consequent emphasis on the role of planning reflects how our discussions, after an early presentation of a management cycle became almost forgotten in the details of entities and communication equipment design, were time and again brought back to the structure of:

- plan an action
- do the action
- review and control the action.

1.2 Layout of the Book

Part II explains in more detail our view of how the three aspects of planning, development and control can best be used in an information systems development environment.

Part III then describes in more detail the nature of, and the work to be done in, each of the main planning activities, which produce the:

- BSP (Business Strategic Plan)
- ISSP (Information Systems Strategic Plan)

- ISTP (Information System Tactical Plan)
- ISPP (Information System Project Plan).

Part IV describes each of the development phases:

- Feasibility
- Analysis
- User Design
- Technical Design.

Implementation and Maintenance are not covered.

Part V describes the main management review and control techniques to be applied.

The final part draws together the main conclusions.

1.3 Phase Description Structure

Each phase is described in a chapter. We usually have the following subheadings:

1	Introduction
2	Framework diagram
3	Definition
4	Objectives
5	Scope
6	Prerequisites
7	Task list
8	Product list
9	Task descriptions
10	Product descriptions
11	Resources
12	Techniques and tools
13	General comments
14	References and sources
15	Project control
16	Ideas and suggestions

1.4 Diagram Conventions

A flow or sequence line where the flow or sequence is down and/or right may be shown with or without an arrowhead. Arrowheads can also be omitted where the line leaves the bottom or right of a box and enters the top or left of another box. Otherwise pointed arrowheads are shown.

Grey and red tones are artistic choice; mostly they carry no meaning.

Red comments are points for you the reader to note; these would not normally appear on a similar diagram being used for communication between knowledgeable experts. The line from such a comment to the object it refers to may be red or black; usually there is a small gap between such a line and the object. Red lines are sometimes used to emphasize something for you.

II PLANNING, DEVELOPMENT AND CONTROL

2 A FRAMEWORK FOR MANAGEMENT

2.1 The Management Cycle

To design, develop and implement a computer-based information system may require many activities - involving many disciplines, techniques and skills. In theory, if all these activities were undertaken by *one ideal* individual then nothing would go wrong, as that individual would understand everything about the system he or she was developing. But the development might take too long, and the ideal individual, if indeed he or she exists, might not be available.

In practice, a computer-based information system is rarely developed by a single individual. Normally a *team* of individuals bring their range of skills, knowledge and experience. A well-coordinated team can complete the system development in a small fraction of the time a single individual would take. However, employing a team presents a different problem, that of **team management**, which means *extra* planning and control, as it is necessary to divide the work out in order to utilize each member of the team. Extra steps must then be taken to ensure that work is carried out in the required manner so that the results integrate properly to construct the desired product.

These steps include extra work to *coordinate* the team members. They must communicate effectively with each other, i.e. have internal discussions and internal documents. And because they work in parallel, each team member must work on the appropriate activities in a satisfactory time sequence.

The quality of the work and the achievement of objectives depend not only on doing the appropriate activities when scheduled, but on the personalities of the people. Having good people is fundamental. They must appreciate human issues and human behaviour as well as technical details.

Management - including planning, review and control - is also needed to ensure that the work of the team progresses satisfactorily from the organization's point of view, fitting its needs and keeping within allocated resources and time.

Good management implies the ability to lead others and work in a team, excellent decisions, integrity, conscientiousness, reliability and achieving objectives.

Team management is not a new problem. It has been successfully addressed by many business organizations. A simple concept is employed to manage a business, known as the **management cycle**. The same management cycle concept can be applied to the work of managing information systems development and this is illustrated in Figure 2.1.

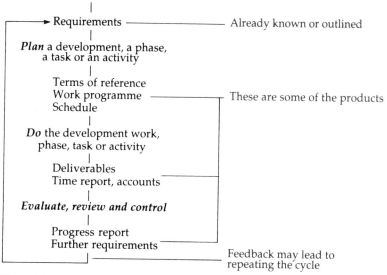

Figure 2.1

The cycle usually *starts* at the **planning process**, where *requirements* may have already been stated or observed. The **plan** will:

- define the scope and objectives of the development process, the *Terms of Reference*
- identify the phases, tasks and activities to be performed and provide estimates for completing them, the *Work Programme*
- establish start and end dates for each of the phases, tasks and activities, the *Schedule*.

Thus the plan will direct the development process, i.e. specify the phases, tasks and activities identified in the work programme. *Completion* of doing any one piece of work is marked by the production of the required end-products, *deliverables*. A deliverable is not necessarily tangible. It is also not necessarily satisfactory. For internal review and control, other products such as time reports and accounts indicate the resources used.

Finally there is the *review and control process*. This is an *ongoing* process requiring the effective employment of the available development resources to ensure that the work is completed on schedule. To ensure that there is no loss of control, key variables, such as the time spent on development activities, the effort required to complete outstanding activities, and the quality of the development work, need to be *monitored*. So *parts* of the review and control occur *during* the period when the work is being done. Other parts of the review and control occur *after* the work has been finished, e.g. reviewing the deliverables to ensure that they satisfy the objectives and goals. The review and control may involve people who were not in the team doing the work, and may generate further requirements from their feedback.

The management cycle is a continual loop, the plan is continually revised in the light of progress to date and changing requirements. Usually one starts from requirements, as drawn above. For a satisfactory outcome at least one cycle must be completed. If one starts anywhere other than at planning then usually one should traverse one's first step (i.e. 'do' or 'review and control') twice.

2.2 Planning for Information Systems

Most people would agree that some planning for information systems (ISs) is essential, but have difficulties over:

- what the planning tasks and activities are
- when, e.g. at which stages they should be done
- how they should be done
- who should do them.

Also, as people often regard planning as a continual process, it cannot be regarded as a discrete phase having discrete tasks. We have resolved these problems as follows.

Firstly, we state that information systems planning (ISP) should go on continually. But for clarity we describe it here as though it were being performed for the first time. This enables easier description of ISP aspects, but you should remember that in practice plans are continually being made, updated, reviewed as progress is monitored, and even abandoned.

Planning is broken down into four types:

- **Business Strategic Planning** (BSP)
- **Information Systems Strategic Planning**, ISSP, which is an extension of BSP, covering the overall planning of information systems
- **Information System Tactical Planning**, ISTP, which relates to the design and development of any *one* information system (IS) or one related group of information systems
- **Planning of any particular phase**, e.g. analysis, or any task or activity within a phase. This Information System Project Planning, ISPP, is like ISTP but in greater detail.

We use the term **ISP** to mean ISSP, ISTP and ISPP. We use BSP and the other acronyms to stand for whichever is needed of:

- 'BS Plan'
- 'BS Planning'

and you should read them as appropriate.

Later chapters discuss these four types of planning, which differ in nature and orientation, but a brief picture here may help. BSP means establishing an organization-wide strategy, with management decisions about trends in the way the organization is to evolve and progress. If the top management strategy is not known and understood then an investigating team may be able to do the minimum to deduce and document the aspects relevant to information systems planning. This should ensure the correct relationship between the organization as a whole, e.g. its overall plans and needs, and the overall conceptual views of its information systems, e.g. not usually involving technical issues.

Organization —— This has BSP and ISSP continually going on

Figure 2.2

ISSP should be the joint responsibility of senior managers in both user departments and computing-oriented or management-services departments, since ISSP concerns identifying, in general terms, the information systems needed to fulfil the strategic plans and needs of the organization. The policies, directions, constraints and resources of the information systems are determined.

ISSP deals with the overall long-term planning and coordination of the various information systems for the organization as a whole. It includes anything requiring a global view, the identification of each information system required, and specification of the structure and terms of reference of each IS. Like BSP, ISSP is only concerned with specifying plans in

Beryl Sanders
MSc BA MInstAM CertEd
Work Placement Tutor (HND)

City of London Polytechnic
84 Moorgate
London EC2M 6SQ
Telephon‌‌‌‌ - -

outline, since the detailed state of the organization and its environment is continually changing.

Each ISTP concerns *one* information system (IS), and coordination of its parts. An individual IS can be large or small and may comprise many related computer applications, e.g. sharing hardware, software and data.

Figure 2.3

At any time each IS should have its current ISTP. Down the years its ISTP may change, due to changes in technology, in the BSP, in the ISSP, or for other reasons. A satisfactory existing IS may have an ISTP which just says 'No changes planned'.

An IS may involve many projects, e.g. changes, developments and ongoing use. Each such project should have its ISPP.

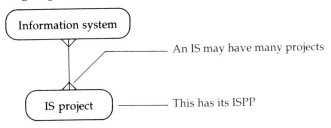

Figure 2.4

You should note that in our framework ISSP applies to information systems, but ISTP and ISPP apply to *one* IS or to part of one IS.

2.3 Information Systems Development

We have constructed a structure to describe the development of information systems. We shall explain it gradually. In it we use the following terms, all of which are for types of things.

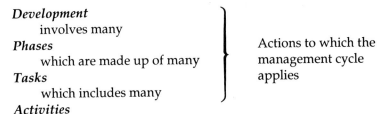

23

Each of the above actions may use many:
Techniques
> which involves using many   Terms about ways
>   of doing actions

Tools

Here 'many' may be none, one or several.

You should notice and distinguish in the above:

• terms for types of actions

• terms concerning ways of doing an action.

We said above that each technique involves many tools. But we did not state the relationship degree in the other direction. Each tool may be used in many techniques. So the relationship is many-to-many. It may be drawn as in Figure 2.5.

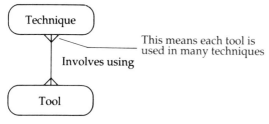

Figure 2.5

You may find an example helpful. Gluing and screwing are techniques. A screwdriver is a tool. A screwdriver may be used either to spread glue or to turn a screw. Information system development techniques and tools are similarly related.

A development may involve applying the management cycle several times, at increasing levels of detail. For example the development of an information system may be structured as in Figure 2.6.

The indented columns correspond to the different levels of our structure of terms.

We use the term **action** for any one of a development, a phase, a task or an activity; in order to describe the various possible sequencing structures in what follows.

You should realize that Figure 2.6 is only an example. It was for one IS, whereas in general the framework may apply to several ISs, or to a change to a part of one IS. Also the wording in a column, 'Plan ..., and for each ... Do ... (and) Review and Control ...' should be generalized. In general the framework allows one or more, or all, of the actions to be planned before the first action is started. The framework does not imply that doing the first action should be finished before the second is started. And in general the points we made in Sections 2.1 and 2.2 apply to each action, e.g. parts of its review and control occur during doing it. In general in our diagrams the flow lines down the page or from left to right usually mean the order in which actions should start, but do not imply priority or finishing one before starting another.

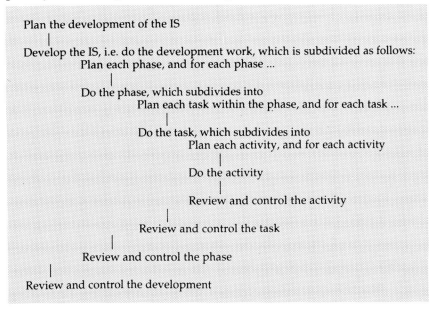

Figure 2.6

Each column in the diagram above for the planning, doing, and reviewing and controlling of an action may be *repeated* in three different ways:

- to refine the current deliverables by repeating the *current* action
- to move from the first to the *next* action and so on till all actions at this level have been done once
- to repeat an *earlier* action at this level in the light of information arising in a later action, or to coordinate and check their products or results.

These three kinds of repetitions may themselves be combined in various ways at each level.

Developers may also **interrupt** a particular action, do part or all of some other action or actions, then return to the interrupted action. The interrupting actions need not be at the same level or of the same type as the interrupted action. Interrupting actions can themselves be interrupted.

The plan for an information system development, or in general for an action, may separate it into several similar actions - one for each of several **areas**. Thus the actions in each area become as far as possible independent: they can be done concurrently, giving the possibility of faster overall progress. The choice of areas might correspond to the different parts of the organization: e.g. based on geographical location; or on division, department and section; or on business functions; or on some other logical grouping.

Whenever an action involves a planning or design decision, e.g. a *choice between alternatives*, it is possible to do the extra action of investigating the *feasibility* of the likely choice or plan. Thus feasibility may be either:

• part of planning
• a stand-alone activity.

In either case it can involve doing a little of various lower-level actions, e.g. to estimate the performance or cost of a proposed information system or proposed design detail.

The end of any management cycle is usually when agreement is reached that the actions have been successful and the objectives achieved effectively. This may follow an evaluation and progress report. This gives a milestone, which means a management checkpoint, or a technical or development highlight.

You should realize that it is possible for a development either to be planned, done and reviewed within a day, or to take a team of several tens of people a couple of years.

2.4 Review and Control

Managers responsible for the investment in a major project may be unwilling to commit all of their resources to a project and then await the delivery of the final product. This mode has risks, so instead most managers like to take things a step at a time. If the project is not going according to plan there is then the opportunity to stop and thus minimize any losses. Alternatively, at any step they may decide to change the product specification to ensure that it can still be developed within an acceptable budget.

For any organization the construction of an information system can be a major investment, so the entire development process is broken into **phases**. At the end of each phase the managers responsible for the investment decisions will be presented with a report of the work completed, a list of available options, and estimates of the costs and benefits associated with each option. Investment decisions, such as those described above, can then be taken between each phase.

To help with such review and control, progress reports may also be produced *during* a long phase, e.g. at regular dates. These reports may include estimates of the likely costs and benefits of the future work. Many managers accept the discipline of scheduling regular meetings, with reports circulated for reading before each meeting.

With any project the difficulty lies in identifying suitable **break points** (between suitable phases). A glance at the many different commercially available methodology products will reveal that professionals cannot agree on how many of these phases there should be and what they should be called. In trying to identify the phases which fall within the scope of our framework we tried to identify the major deliverables which would be of interest to managers responsible for the investment decisions. After some iteration we identified the following as **observable deliverables** giving major break points between phases:

- a report on the likely benefits and costs of the entire project
- a project plan
- a statement of requirements in detail
- a model of the system, i.e. a description of the proposed system's main facilities and features from the users' viewpoint
- a complete specification of the system
- a working system.

The feasibility report is sometimes omitted, particularly for small projects or where people can easily judge the feasibility. We were able to identify appropriate phases, with the above as the main deliverables.

After each phase, and, where appropriate, on a regular basis during a phase, higher management should review progress and the quality of the work performed. Thus the managers may:

- give approval to go ahead with the next phase as previously planned
- give approval to go ahead with the next phase, but subject to qualifications, policy changes and new directives
- request further work to be done, maybe of the type in a past phase that is now judged not entirely satisfactory
- request a review, further planning, feasibility evaluation
- request more details of progress, or auditing of it
- delay, curtail, reduce or stop the project
- start a different project.

2.5 The Management of the Planning

The day-to-day *management* tasks such as the scheduling, reviewing and controlling of ongoing services are *not* part of ISSP. Such management should be applied to all phases and tasks, including to the carrying out of ISSP.

Later chapters give the objectives, tasks and products for BSP, ISSP, ISTP and ISPP. In principle each such planning task should itself be planned, done, reviewed and controlled in a management cycle for that task. Sometimes such a management cycle will degenerate:

- its planning may be trivial or nearly so - the people involved should make good use of their time and of other resources
- its review may perhaps be just a discussion that agrees that the planning task was done satisfactorily, so its delivered products are accepted, and these products may form part of the input to other planning tasks
- the review of the plans as a whole may be a meeting which approves the plans produced.

2.6 Framework Application

The framework has been constructed in such a way as to accommodate different development approaches. To a large extent this has been achieved by specifying what the **prerequisites** for individual phases of development are, rather than specifying the sequence in which these phases should be performed. We shall illustrate various approaches by diagrams of their main phases.

The traditional **life-cycle** approach to systems development is supported as follows. Some methodologies use slightly different terms for the phases. The meaning of the lines between the phases is explained below Figure 2.8.

The comments on the right in Figure 2.7 apply similarly to all our framework application diagrams in this section.

In the traditional life-cycle approach each phase in Figure 2.7 is usually treated as a separate project and each such project must be finished before the next starts. If the organization is divided into areas, then the whole development may be planned so that the diagram applies separately to each area, but with appropriate coordination across areas. You should interpret the lines in the diagram to mean all that, but after the next such diagram we shall further generalize the scheduling.

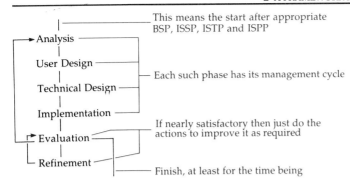

Figure 2.7

The **prototyping** approach to systems development is supported as shown in Figure 2.8.

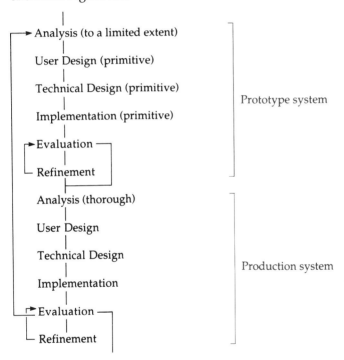

Figure 2.8

Figure 2.8 shows two stages, prototype system and production system. In practice there may be more than two such stages. In each stage a new version of some or all of the products is created, being a significant improvement. Where no changes are needed, appropriate parts of a prototype version may or may not be used in the next version.

The following comments apply to the prototyping diagram in Figure 2.8 and to the remaining diagrams of this section:

- The relevant *BSP, ISSP and ISTP should be completed before the first phase*, e.g. Analysis, starts.

- The relevant *ISPP should be completed before each phase starts*, if a phase is a project. Where a project covers several areas or phases, the relevant ISPP for that part should be completed before its actions start.

- Where an action, e.g. an analysis task, should produce a product that is a *prerequisite* to some other action, say a UD or TD task, then the *first action should be started and should produce a primitive version of the product before the second action starts*. This is the **prerequisite rule**.

- If an IS development is subdivided into areas, then that prerequisite rule applies as appropriate separately to each action for each area. Appropriate *cross-coordination* across areas, through prerequisites, together with appropriate planning, review and control is assumed.

- In principle the whole diagram can occur for *each* IS development. The words 'In principle' imply avoiding unnecessary repetition of actions:
  - where a product already exists from a previous IS development
  - where a previous product can be adapted or amended if that is simpler than repeating the previous action in full.

- **Evaluation** includes developmental testing or real use by end-users or their representatives, or by an equivalent quality control team or audit team. Where evaluation, feedback from users or other comment suggests a minor improvement, then this may be added by thinking it out and making a refinement. Such a refinement may have a nearly trivial management cycle. Its actions are only those parts of previous tasks that are needed for the change and to maintain consistency between deliverables.

- The *repetition* up the left from an evaluation indicates actions that will have to be partly repeated if the evaluation shows that a major product is grossly unsatisfactory, or if new requirements imply major changes.

The **incremental** approach to systems development means that features are gradually added one after another; similarly use of a system may be gradually extended into more areas of an organization. Suppose most of the features being added arise from improving User Design aspects, e.g. easier use by better man-machine interface details like commands and screen layouts. Then the analysis products are not affected.

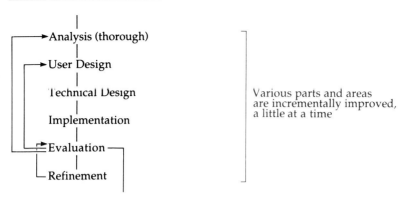

Figure 2.9

As more powerful tools such as application generators and better data dictionary facilities become increasingly available, the IS developers and users can concentrate more on user design. The automated technical design and implementation is repeated to give the new version of the appropriate products, using as defaults all the decisions incorporated into the previous version of the product. Maybe in the future the users and developers might have such powerful tools that even more of UD and TD might be automated, so that when the users or developers think of an analysis change, its consequences, including new commands, screen layouts and other man-machine interface features, will be automatically incorporated into the next version of the products affected.

Our final example in this section illustrates how *two* information systems could *share* the analysis of requirements. The tactical separation between them is then made on some criterion that results from the analysis products. Thereafter each of the two separate information systems will have its own ISTP. There are thus three projects: the analysis; the first IS's UD, TD...; and the second IS's UD, TD... Each such project will have its ISPP. In practice an organization might have far more than three such projects.

Parallel development of two ISs that share analysis is supported as in Figure 2.10, where for simplicity some flow lines are omitted.

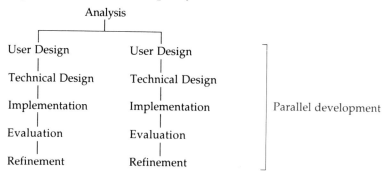

Figure 2.10

In general the prototyping, incremental and parallel development approaches above can be *combined*. Our purpose here is to illustrate how the various phases can be scheduled, by relating them through prerequisites.

Different tasks and activities within a phase and between phases can be similarly related through prerequisites. Separate IS developments, on the other hand, are usually not related through such prerequisites: they are related in a different way through the BSP and ISSP of the organization. The above examples illustrate the framework within which fit various possible sequences of actions. They do *not* illustrate the fundamental differences in philosophy and assumptions on which the approaches are based.

2.7 The Role of Tools and Techniques

We regard techniques and tools as secondary to phases, tasks and activities for two reasons:

- the overall goals of the organization are usually translated more easily into developments, with phases, tasks and activities, than into statements about techniques and tools
- new techniques and tools are constantly being made available to information system developers.

Tools and techniques may span one, several or all phases. Developers should think mainly about the phases, tasks and activities, then secondarily about appropriate tools and techniques for the required phases, tasks and activities.

We believe that a framework in which tools and techniques are subordinate is more likely to stand the course of time, as experience has shown that tools and techniques change more rapidly than the set of tasks and activities carried out to develop information systems. However, we recognize that the availability of certain tools - such as data dictionaries, software workbenches and application generators - has led to major rethinks about the way in which systems are developed.

III PLANNING

3 BUSINESS STRATEGIC PLANNING

Planning is a vital activity. In particular it is necessary:

- to coordinate and make decisions about the overall direction and aims of the organization, i.e. at the *corporate level*, which is the subject of this chapter
- to give a *strategy* for the organization and thus for all the organization's *information systems*
- to plan each *information system*
- to plan each *project*, e.g. phase of development of each information system.

Planning is an activity with several facets:

- breakdown of a future project into more-easily manageable units such as a network of actions, which include phases, tasks and activities, and which are linked by suitable events for review and control; i.e. deciding *how* the whole is to be done
- scheduling *when* each such action should occur
- *estimating* for each action the **resources** involved, which may be either used or created or transformed from one form to another, e.g. income, expenditure, capital assets, plant, materials, labour
- *allocating* the appropriate resources to each action, e.g. picking particular staff with the required skills, suitable equipment and tools
- deciding the **method of managing** each action, including *how* its leadership, decision making, review and control should be done
- *decision making* on policies, constraints, alternatives; which may translate into **directives** to those who take action; this is both part of management at a higher level and planning for the future actions at a lower level
- ensuring the *feasibility* of the plans, policy and directives.

Project management includes the day-to-day or month-by-month management cycle of monitoring, feedback, evaluation of progress and consequential replanning. Further planning activity, producing revised plans, and other decision making may be needed as a result of either progress evaluation or external information.

3.1 Introduction to Business Strategic Planning

Business strategic planning (BSP) is part of corporate planning. BSP translates the corporate objectives into key policy decisions. Part of BSP should determine the role and place of information systems (ISs) in the organization, including an overall allocation of resources in accordance with the corporate budget. In organizations where a BSP may *not* be readily or wholly available a small fact-finding team should ascertain the relevant aspects of corporate strategy, particularly those BSP aspects relevant to information systems.

3.2 Framework Diagram for BSP

Figure 3.1 outlines the main tasks of business strategic planning.

Each **box** in Figure 3.1 is a task or group of actions in the logical sequence of tasks and in principle could be broken down into activities in a critical path analysis network. In practice such a critical path analysis would not be likely to be very useful.

Each **line** represents that one activity should *start* before a second one is started, but does *not* imply that the first should finish before the second either starts or finishes. Thus the lines do not represent the same as the relationships in critical path analysis, where each activity starts at an event and finishes at another event. The activities here are usually iterative, with information flows between them. For definiteness we have chosen to illustrate a manufacturing context.

The **upper half** of the diagram concerns the organization as a whole.

The **upper left side** of the diagram is concerned with the state and trends of the main factors affecting the organization's business. Analysis of Strengths, Weaknesses, Opportunities, Threats (SWOT) for each Plant, Product, Price, Person, Place, Performance, Productivity, Policy, Penny, ...(a matrix structure). (**SWOT for each P.**)

The **right side** concerns decisions and the flow of information, decisions about management and control, e.g. whether control is centralized or devolved, the relative importance of ISs, and the consequences for information systems strategy plus, development and use.

The activities at the **lower left**, though usually the main stream of the manufacturing business, do not form part of BSP relevant to information systems strategy, but these decisions and their consequences flow as information. So the ISs need facilities to handle them, their products and feedback.

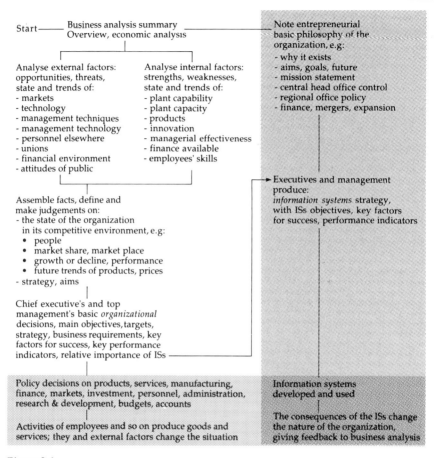

Figure 3.1

The **middle right** shows that executives and top management, possibly in consultation with middle managers, analysts and consultants, should produce an information systems strategic plan. Plans and developments of each information system should follow. Evaluation of the effects of earlier such developments should produce feedback concerning:

- external factors such as demand for goods and services
- internal factors such as improved decision making, production scheduling and productivity.

A 'top manager' of an organization that does not have a BSP may ask a consultancy to help develop its information systems plans, or may ask some of its own middle or senior managers to draw up such plans. The **investigating team** of consultants or managers may be able to persuade the top manager to allow them to spend, say, a couple of weeks or months - to identify the relevant BSP aspects. This **relevant minimum**

BSP approach is described below. We shall use the term **top management** to mean whichever is appropriate of director, executive, board member and senior manager.

The tasks and activities of the investigating team are summarized in Figure 3.2.

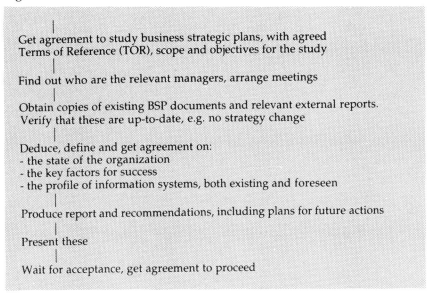

|
Get agreement to study business strategic plans, with agreed
Terms of Reference (TOR), scope and objectives for the study
|
Find out who are the relevant managers, arrange meetings
|
Obtain copies of existing BSP documents and relevant external reports.
Verify that these are up-to-date, e.g. no strategy change
|
Deduce, define and get agreement on:
- the state of the organization
- the key factors for success
- the profile of information systems, both existing and foreseen
|
Produce report and recommendations, including plans for future actions
|
Present these
|
Wait for acceptance, get agreement to proceed

Figure 3.2

Various alternative decisions were listed near the end of Section 2.4.

3.3 Definition of BSP

The aim of business strategic planning is to develop and document top management plans, taking into account the organization's current and future needs, internal and external trends, and all policy aspects. This should yield organization-wide objectives. This process should be continually going on among top management.

The aim of the **relevant minimum** business strategic planning is to develop and document those aspects of the top management plans of the organization that are needed as a *basis for an information systems strategy* that takes account of the current and future needs of the organization through a targeted identification of the relevant facts, trends and organizational objectives. This includes the decision-making processes and structures.

If consultants are involved, then this minimum business strategic planning may be carried out during the initial period of contact with top management in response to an invitation to discuss problems and requirements. Consultants and managers responsible for information systems should occasionally check that their understanding of the organization's BSP is correct and up-to-date, and where appropriate carry out a BSP review or repeat the relevant minimum BSP.

3.4 Objectives of BSP

At the end of the relevant minimum business strategic planning the appropriate managers and investigating team should have proper understanding and widespread agreement over those aspects of the organization's overall plans that may affect information systems provision and development.

The BSP should cover an agreed time horizon, stating quantified observable objectives against which the overall performance of the organization can be measured. A long term plan should state a target organizational pattern, say ten years hence. This may be developed into more detailed medium term targets that lie on an appropriate development path from the present situation towards the long term pattern. The plans should allow flexibility for change and evolution when unexpected factors arise.

The **relevant minimum** BSP includes understanding and documentation of:

- the organization in its competitive environment
- medium term trends, for example the past three years and the next three years
- key factors for success
- summary of existing and likely future information system requirements.

The overall objective of the relevant minimum BSP is to produce and maintain an outline plan for the provision and development of information systems for the organization. The plan should cover current and future objectives over an agreed time horizon.

This should result in the following BSP documents:

1   The organization in its competitive environment.
2   Corporate outline policy statement on information systems strategy.

3   Reports on:
   - existing and future decision-making processes, planning and control
   - existing information systems strategy, objectives, performance, and future hopes and expectations
   - top management's perceived issues that may suggest changes such as new information systems and improvements.
4   Phase-end report - including outline plans for and recommendations to proceed with particular developments, or recommend to review further, or to abort particular developments.

The phase end should include appropriate presentations of these documents.

3.5 Scope of BSP

Essentially BSP is concerned with the identification of future hopes and expectations by top management, contrasting these with the projections of the organization's past performance and deciding appropriate courses of action in general terms.

In the relevant minimum BSP approach the scope will be limited to those aspects of the organization's planning that may affect existing and future information systems during their expected life.

Usually there is a **gap** between the future hopes, intentions and expectations and the trend of actual recent past performance which the top management of the organization will want to close. This should lead to the identification of the *key factors for success* in closing the gap. The relevant minimum approach will be limited to those key factors for success that involve the organization's strategies for information systems and computers.

For clarification, the scope of some of the documents listed in Section 3.4 is listed briefly.

1 The organization in its competitive environment
The scope includes obtaining data, graphs and statements to enable key factors for success and performance-expectations gaps to be identified. Preferably avoid getting involved in making forecasts, analysing or editing accounts, and so on.

2 *Corporate outline policy statement on information systems strategy*

All the business functions in all areas of the organization should be briefly considered. For each function that may require or is already served by computerized information systems the relevant priorities, resources, strengths and weaknesses that may affect ISSP should be stated. Other functions not requiring computers usually need only be listed to show that they have not been accidentally omitted from consideration.

3 *Other reports*

The reports on existing and required information systems, strategy, performance and top management's perceived issues should include: measurable objectives, priorities, desirable time-scales and resources, goals, targets, trends and developments in information technology that may significantly affect the organization. But preferably restrict what is reported at this phase to information that top management needs to know about or should be aware of. What information the top management needs should be deduced from its policy and decision-making process. Avoid details, particularly technical details, that are not needed for top management decisions, and that can be deferred. What is researched may be wider in scope than what is reported: further information will thus be known which can give justifications if questions are asked at the top management presentation.

4 *Phase-end report*

A recommendation to abort is rare, but may be the only prudent thing to do. The investigating team must make the scope of their work sufficiently wide and thorough to be absolutely certain of their recommendations. Any doubts should be investigated in greater detail and thus resolved. People whose recommendations become flawed lose acceptability: we return to this in Section 3.13.

3.6 Prerequisites of BSP

The following is a minimum list of prerequisites for the relevant minimum approach:

1   Agreement from top management to enter into strategic planning.

2   Agreement with top management to carry out the necessary tasks: interviews, briefings and fact finding. This includes a specific list of names, and job titles, of senior managers and executives to be contacted. Obviously they must cooperate enthusiastically.

3   An outline history of recent, say three years', performance and environment must be available. For a manufacturing company this should include annual reports and accounts, industry reports *(Financial Times, The Economist, Investors' Chronicle*, for example), and interfirm comparisons for the company, or at least for the industry sector.

In this phase statutory laws, auditing policy, data protection policy, and so on, are part of the internal and external environment of the organization. Understanding and description of these form part of the objectives of this phase.

4   Where external consultants or any middle managers new to the organization's strategic planning are involved there should be a pre-engagement briefing of the investigating team, covering the above and explaining the objectives.

3.7 Task List

1   Define the *state of the organization* in its competitive environment: internal and external. E.g. *SWOT for each P* as in Section 3.2.

2   Deduce and agree with the top management the *key factors for success* for the organization for the strategic-plan time-horizon.

3   Define the *profile* of the existing information and data-processing systems.

4   Define the top management *objectives* for the existing information systems.

5   Define any *gap* between the trend of recent past performance and the hopes, intentions and expectations of the existing information systems.

6   Identify the main *relevant issues* and alternatives.

7   Agree with top management their *priorities* for organizational requirements that involve information systems requirements for the planning time-horizon ahead.

8   Write the end of phase *report*: this may give recommendations such as to proceed to a next phase or to review initial ideas with executives.

9   Discuss the setting up of a *steering group*, committee or party for 'strategic planning reviews'.

10   Design and prepare visual aids. Rehearse an end of phase presentation of the documents. Plan and execute the *presentation.*

3.8 Major Products

The major products of this phase are divided into two classes:

1   **Reports** for the top executives and senior management.

2   **Appraisals** by the investigating team that they keep *confidential* to themselves.

The **products**, e.g. reports for top management, and all with styles and contents to fit the decision-making processes, should cover:

- the state of the organization in its competitive environment - key factors for success
- corporate outline policy statement on information systems strategy
- the existing information systems: manual, computerized
- new systems and improvements: requirements at corporate level only
- recommendations: proceed or review
- formal presentation of the reports.

The **internal appraisals**, confidential to the investigating team, are:

- records of interviews and briefings
- progress and outcome reports on task execution
- conclusions from this phase.

The SWOT analysis with all its details and reasons, might not be needed or appropriate as a product to be presented, but it should be available if requested.

3.9 Task Descriptions

1 Define the state of the organization in its competitive environment. Ideally this may be obtained readily from top managers. Otherwise in practice the team must do fact-finding interviews and study whatever documents are available, to discover for each area of the organization the present and projected future position. For example in a manufacturing company this should cover:

(i)   **Internal factors**:

- state of plant technology, capacity, capability
- research and development, product innovation, market trends
- managerial effectiveness, techniques, technology, age distribution, adaptability, morals

- work force: union memberships, age structure, skills, adaptability, morals
- plant locations and distribution centres with respect to markets.

The internal factors also include the following entrepreneurial factors:

- basic philosophy of the organization at the key management levels: Board, Chief Executive, executives, middle management
- what types of control are tightly held centrally, what types are delegated to regional and line management, what boards and committees exist with what terms of reference
- specific objectives, goals and targets: detailed enough for information systems strategy
- plans: success rate of past plans, current plans.

(ii) **External factors**:

- markets: share, location, characteristics
- technology: products, marketing, distribution
- management techniques, technology, attitudes
- interest groups: government, trade unions, consumers, shareholders
- legal developments, courts and professions.

2 Define, with top management, key factors for success to achieve stated corporate objectives, goals and targets. Each key factor for success and each objective should be stated in terms that can be observed, or measured in quantified ways at specified dates or calculated as a performance indicator.

3 Define and describe briefly the profile of existing information systems, both computerized and manual, in terms of their successes, problems, assets, technology, manpower, history and plans. Here 'existing' includes anything for which decisions have been made and resources committed, even if not yet implemented. The top management view is required.

4 Define and describe briefly the objectives, goals and targets of the existing information systems as seen by top management, including representative user management.

5 Define and describe briefly any gap between recent past performance and future hopes and expectations from the existing information systems, manual and computerized, as perceived by top and user management.

6 Identify and describe briefly the main issues, as seen by top management. These issues may be areas of the organization that have problems or seem to be in some way an unsatisfactory muddle. For example the organization's top plans may include moving into new products, new engineering or production methods, new financial or legal situations, and new methods of sales and marketing. The continual improvements in computer, control and automation technology may affect the organization, e.g. its internal methods of operation and management, the external customer demand for its products and services, and its external suppliers. For each issue there may be alternatives. These may include or lead to more or fewer employees; higher or lower use of computer and other technology; and higher or lower expenditure, income, investment and assets. Top management should be able to list those issues and main alternatives, or at least the relevant minimum needed for information systems planning.

7 Define the priorities, together with criteria and desirable time-scales, for each organizational requirement. This means corporate organizational objectives, not information systems ones. The information system's priorities come in ISSP.

8 Write the report on strategic planning, outlining overall feasibility and limitations of requirements, stating next steps - proceed or review - and stating the necessary organization commitments for the next phases.

9 Consider whether to recommend that top management should set up a **group** or **steering** party or committee for 'strategic planning reviews'. If so think out justification and plan.

10 Prepare and give appropriate presentations to key organization executives and user and computer management on the recommendations and next steps.

The objective of a formal presentation is to gain acceptance of the main recommendations at the end of a phase of work. This is followed by handing over the actual reports to the executives and managers concerned.

The preparations include discussing and deciding the programme and the roles of the various individuals, e.g. for each point who is the best person to explain it. The discussion should identify which executives have key opinions and which are key decision makers. Maybe some of the main points should be explained to certain executives individually in private before the formal presentation, so those executives have understood the synthesis and thus may help guide the discussion at the presentation rather than asking awkward or sidetracking questions.

The task includes making arrangements such as room booking and refreshments, after enquiries leading to a choice of date fitting all the required executives and managers. Visual aids need preparing. The whole needs rehearsal.

3.10 Major Products Detailed Description

3.10.1 Top Executive and Senior Management Reports

1 The state of the organization in its competitive environment - key factors for success

This document must define in the briefest possible way the essential achievements within defined time and budgetary limits that the organization must realize if it is to close the gap between its expectations and future plans, and past performance. Each business area must be covered, and also the relationships and links between areas.

2 Corporate outline policy statement on information systems strategy

This is essentially a high level plan detailing the functions and scope of each major system and how they address the business requirements of the organization. Its style should be appropriate to top management. Further details will evolve and be added at the later information systems planning phases. Some activities that belong to ISSP and other phases may be required to ensure accuracy and feasibility.

The scope and the interaction of the systems must be specified, together with their development priorities under the projected plans of the business, followed by the allocation of resources in terms of personnel, finance, training and equipment, highlighting the organizational strengths and weaknesses of the plans made.

Example

The following is a shortened example:

'All existing computerized information systems perform well, in total costing about 0.5 percent of turnover, which is acceptable. User departments are generally fully happy with the services provided. The following systems are needed in this priority:

- sales management system
- decision support system for costing
- distributed stock control system.

The resources required for the development of the sales management system are about 20 man-months, 40 percent of the total staff time and 35 percent of the total budget for these projects.

On priorities versus feasibility, the decision support system for costing is more urgent than the sales management system, but cannot be properly developed until the other systems are implemented. So, as a short-term expedient, a package will be used for costing, taking up about 10 percent of the total budget. Although this package may have to be discarded or modified when the new system is built, the investment may be recouped through the experience gained, the value to the organization as a whole of earlier and better costing decisions, and the quality of decision making relevant to the other systems.'

3 Other reports

There may be one or more brief reports that together cover the other items listed in Sections 3.4, 3.5 and 3.8 that reports for top management should cover. Details and style may depend on the organization, its personalities, objectives, recent performance, future expectations, issues and other things we mentioned in the Section 3.9 task descriptions.

4 Recommendations - proceed or review

This document puts forward the investigating team's formal recommendations on how to proceed to the next phase or whether to review the initial program and assumptions with the organization's executives and senior management.

Essentially this is a 'next steps' document, which must specify the inputs required from the organization as a prerequisite for proceeding to the next phase, or in the case of a review state the reasons for the review.

3.10.2 Internal Appraisals - Confidential to the Investigating Team

The investigating team may have discussions amongst themselves about the extent to which each management executive agrees the various aspects of the strategy. Such discussion may be not minuted. These appraisals are stated in Section 3.8. They are likely to vary in detailed format and structure from project to project, and depend on the personality of the team managers.

3.11 Resources

Broadly speaking, the resource requirements in this phase are an investigating team including appropriate experience of management and information system development; together with some other senior managers' time; and some costs.

The investigating team should:

- have broad experience in quick investigations into defining the business performance of organizations
- be effective from shop-floor to boardroom in communications

- be proficient analytically in the technical skills of analysis, and synthesis, such as accounting and finance, forecasting, interpretation of company ratios, planning and control techniques, such as PERT
- be a good judge of managerial abilities
- have a grasp of key points of hardware and software development, sufficient understanding of computer technology and techniques to work effectively with the computer systems analyst on this stage, and preferably on the feasibility study stage as well
- be skilful in handling personal relations at all levels
- be experienced in quickly and correctly translating business systems requirements into an outline of computer systems
- have an in-depth grasp of computer systems and languages, be they mainframe, mini or micro systems, and be fully aware of the cost and time-scale problems of systems from the strategic planning stage to implementation
- be able to envisage alternative hardware and software configurations to fit the functions, circumstances and personalities of the user managers
- be understanding and sympathetic to the business problems and information requirements of the non-technical user
- be capable of devising a computer strategy from the information requirement plans of the organization.

The team will need to inspire confidence in all executives and managers, minimizing the interference with their daily work by conducting their fact-finding interviews in a planned, structured way, keeping records of those events (see Section IV).

Cost and time estimates will vary from project to project. There will be costs be incurred to obtain information for business analysis purposes, such as company accounts, specialist research reports, interfirm comparisons, which may run to several hundred pounds (1988). Costs of computers and word processors may be hidden.

3.12 Techniques and Tools

Business analysis tools and techniques are far too numerous to attempt to describe here. A one-volume reference, 'The Businessman's Complete Checklist' [SHAW78], provides sufficient detailed points on all organizational aspects for an initial plan of investigation to be carried out, as well as to provoke an investigating team to formulate questions of their own in addition to those raised in this book.

3.13 General Comments

The business strategic planning phase calls for a combination of skills, experience, personal abilities and a capacity for quick and decisive thinking. It is quite conceivable that the resources and time available for strategic planning may be extremely limited. The time allotted includes the writing of the reports, which is sometimes underestimated. Illustrations take thought and time, as do preparations for good presentations.

Usually some privacy and confidentiality is important. This implies personal integrity and physical security of documents - e.g. care over disposal of obsolete drafts, and procedures for communication. Those involved should not discuss confidential matters where they may be overheard. Sometimes where someone is, or who that person is with, should not be revealed in a seemingly casual telephone enquiry to a secretary. The credibility and acceptability of the team members may be at stake.

The evolving plans may include potential organizational structure changes: e.g. to departments, divisions, sections and groups, and to the way certain people operate. The possibilities for such changes must be discovered and presented in acceptable ways. Half-baked ideas must not leak out. Tact may be needed to ascertain what is acceptable. The ability to listen counts. Top management must decide how decisions from acceptable recommendations are communicated to those involved.

This chapter describes the relevant minimum for a team investigating a medium to large organization lacking good BSP. Smaller organizations perhaps do not want or cannot afford the overheads and resources. Some organizations may have plans but their top management may wish to retain confidentiality and control - which are not the same, and restrict what information is divulged to middle managers and the BSP project team. And vice-versa middle managers and consultants may be inhibited from saying what they feel, e.g. for fear of losing their jobs and contracts. BSP can be fraught with human-relation problems as well as those of effective communication.

3.14 References and Sources

ALLE79: Brandt Allen. Computer Strategy: A Philosophy for Managing Information Processing Resources. *Organizations and Data Processing* (1979) pp7-18. University of Virginia.

ANON85: *The Manager's Handbook*. Arthur Young & Co., Accountants. Sphere Books. (1985).

JAY70: Antony Jay. *Effective Presentations: the communication of ideas by words and visual aids*. Management Publications Ltd for BIM (1970). ISBN 0-85118-071-X.

PETE88: T. Peters. Thriving On Chaos. Macmillan (1988). An extract on 'Winning the quality war' was published in *The Sunday Times*, 14 Feb. 1988.

SHAW78: S.C. Shaw and G.J. Day. *The Businessman's Complete Checklist*. Business Books (Hutchinson) (1978).

3.16 Ideas and Suggestions

- With colleagues think out, argue out and analyse your whole organization or your part of your organization - SWOT on each product, service, resource ...
- With colleagues, discuss and draw up a marketing plan for your organization; or for the products and services produced by your area.
- How are they measured?
- How are they analysed?
- What is the culture of your organization or your area?
- To what extent are decisions made centrally or delegated. What kinds of decisions are which? Is the pattern the same at lower levels?
- What are the key factors for your organization's success or your area?
- Draw up aims, goals, mission statement, objectives.
- Assess the value of ISs and IT in your organization's corporate planning - to what extent are these central to the business as a whole, or to your area?

4 INFORMATION SYSTEMS STRATEGIC PLANNING

4.1 Introduction to Information Systems Planning

This chapter covers ISSP, i.e. planning for the totality of all information systems in an organization. The next chapter covers tactical planning for each information system, ISTP. The following chapter discusses information system project planning, ISPP. These three together form Information Systems Planning (ISP).

Generally we shall not include in our descriptions of the various development phases and tasks any description of the planning of that phase or task. The general principles of good planning and management should be applied to all phases, tasks and activities.

This includes general principles such as:
- deciding how to manage each unit
- decision making
- directives
- ensuring feasibility
- the management cycle
- scheduling
- resource allocation
- review and control.

Hereafter we assume these without repetition in each chapter.

Of course whereas planning a large phase or task of an information system development may take many days and create many documents, planning a single activity might be just a brief discussion.

4.2 Framework Diagram for ISSP

Information Systems Strategic Planning, ISSP, follows on from the early stages of Business Strategic Planning and usually overlaps with later more detailed aspects of BSP. However, ISSP does not occur in the same timeframe as the analysis and design phases of any particular information system development. Certain aspects of ISSP may operate in parallel with these phases. Figure 4.1 is therefore only an illustrative representation of ISSP.

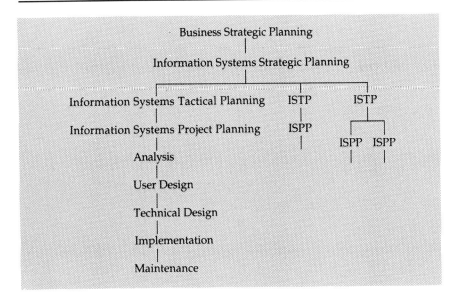

Figure 4.1

The flow lines have the same meaning as in Section 2.6. For clarity this diagram is an example for an organization with three ISs, the third having two projects. Details of phases for the second and third projects are not shown: any pattern from Section 2.6 could appear.

In any one organization ISSP should go on continually and, with shorter timeframes, so should ISTP for each IS.

ISSP, ISTP and other planning activities usually involve a process of iterative refinement, just like any other activity. Circumstances change, experience and understanding is gained, and further information becomes available.

Figure 4.2 illustrates the tasks for the ISSP team. Some of these tasks are continually ongoing and the tasks interact with each other, so the diagram does not imply a time sequence of finishing one task before starting the next. The meaning is as in the comments that follow the prototyping diagram, Figure 2.8 in Section 2.6.

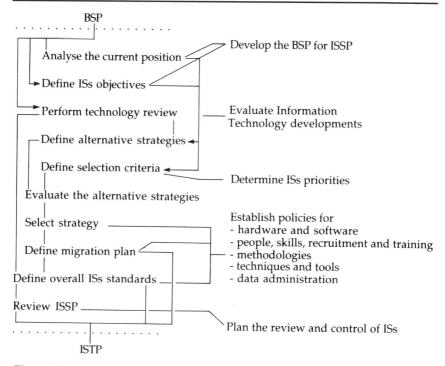

Figure 4.2

4.3 Definition of ISSP

The purpose of ISSP is to produce an overall strategy that coordinates all information systems of the organization. We use the term **global** to mean covering and integrating the whole, or all relevant parts.

Each IS, or group of related such systems, is identified, giving the structure of the next level down.

Long-term plans for what is to be computerized, what should be manual - i.e. not computerized - what has potential for future development, and broad estimates of resources and manpower are reviewed, coordinated and agreed.

Terms of reference (TOR) for each IS are defined, with an outline of the potential benefits, budgets, time-scales and fundamental decisions. **Global** decisions, e.g. about any organization-wide data model, organization-wide data administration, IS standards, hardware and software procurement and development policy, and the planning and management of all these, belong to ISSP. The advantages of coherent organization-wide planning of information systems strategy should be recognized and achieved, rather than letting unsatisfactory inconsistent and incompatible systems grow by default.

4.4 Objective of ISSP

The primary objective of ISSP is to create an environment which facilitates the development of information systems and the integration of the information systems into a coherent whole. This should ensure that the objectives of the information systems, both individually and together, are met as fully as possible. This should result in satisfaction not just with each system, but also with the totality of which each IS is a part.

4.5 Scope of ISSP

Information Systems Strategic Planning (ISSP) is not a discrete, tangible function but a multi-variable activity. The scope is therefore complex. Two sets of factors determine the scope of ISSP in an organization. One is the organizational make-up: such as the size of the business, complexity of product and service lines, management styles, structure and decision making, and the position of the business in its industry class. Second is the reliance upon information systems: for organizations with heavy reliance, like banks, airlines, automated distribution and manufacture, and so on, ISs are of strategic importance and therefore require extensive planning. By contrast, where each IS merely supports routine secondary activities, such as payroll, that are not the main business, ISSP will remain small. Then many of the tasks and products described later in this chapter will hardly be required or appropriate.

The ISSP scope therefore should relate to the roles that the individual ISs have in the organization and on their stages of life. The ISSP team should recognize that these roles may change and therefore they may need to be re-evaluated at intervals.

ISP is an aggregate of three types of planning functions, ISSP, ISTP and ISPP. These three planning functions further sub-divide. ISs for *business functions* need **usage planning**, planning the methods and patterns of use. This differs from planning the *methods of development* of ISs for effective information system development and management.

The **ISSP scope** must appropriately cover:
- clear statement of the objectives of the information systems and applications being developed and their 'acceptance' criteria: this includes both functional objectives such as user's requirements and

53

development objectives such as resources, budgets and time-scales available

- development standards
- appropriate tools and techniques
- suitable training for developers and users [MCFA83].

Irrespective of the extent of planning, the need to perform the three types of ISP cannot be overstated. Commercial organizations rely heavily on information.

4.6 Prerequisites of ISSP

There will be some overlap between this ISSP phase and the business strategic planning phase. As such, some prerequisites specified may be considered as the tasks of the phase while some tasks may be considered as prerequisites. The **prerequisites for ISSP** will be:

- agreement to proceed with ISSP, including the formation of a team for ISSP who accept it as their job and have appropriate review and reporting structures and access to relevant information
- business strategic planning or the relevant minimum for information systems
- statement of the relevant corporate business objectives of the organization
- statement of the business-oriented objectives of the information systems and their correspondence to the business objectives of the organization
- statement of the financial and personnel resource allocation for ISs.

The above should be deducible from meetings, briefings and full understanding of:

- the state of the organization in its competitive environment
- corporate statement of key factors for success of the organization
- corporate statement on ISs strategy, including corporate views on existing ISs, new ISs and improvements
- recommendations and decisions from BSP.

Information confidential to the BSP investigating team may be needed by the ISSP team.

Success requires continuous trust and continual flows of information between top management, the BSP team and the ISSP team.

4.7 Task List for ISSP

The order of this list does not imply the action sequence. Each task may be done continually, i.e. with intermittent review and updating whenever appropriate. The tasks may interact.

1   Analyse the Current Position
   - Develop Profile of the Existing Information Systems
   - Perform Data Review
   - Perform Systems Audit
2   Define Information System Objectives
   - Business Requirements
   - User Requirements
3   Perform Technology Review
4   List and Describe Alternative Strategies
5   Define Selection Criteria
6   Evaluate Alternative Strategies
7   Select Strategy
8   Define Migration Plan
9   Define Overall Information System Standards
10   Review ISSP.

4.8 Major Products List for ISSP

Any of the following may be omitted if not required or appropriate.

- Existing IS profile
   - functional charts (overview)
   - responsibility and involvement matrices
   - global data models
   - system audit report
- Statement of the IS objectives
- Technology and methods review
- Development strategy reports
- Statement of selection criteria
- Strategy evaluation report
- Strategy selection report
- Migration plan
- Component IS report, i.e. list each individual component IS and justification

- For each IS component identified:
  - Terms of Reference
- Statement of IS standards
- Policy statements on e.g.:
  - Hardware and software acquisition policy and plans
  - Development methods
  - Standards
  - Skills acquisition
- Position statements on e.g.:
  - new developments
  - organizational impact
  - existing skills

The above includes:

- Information Systems Development Plans, i.e. a list of the ISs, their priorities and the TOR for each IS. New systems and improvements.
- Report on the impact of ISs on organizational structure and management
- Retrospective report on the costs and benefits of using existing ISs.

4.9 Task Descriptions for ISSP

Section 4.13 contains qualifying remarks that apply to these task descriptions.

1 Analyse the Current Position

The objective of this task is to determine where the organization is in terms of its current information systems provision, whether each part be manual or computerized. This means to identify strengths and weaknesses and particularly to assess the degree to which the existing ISs meet the objectives laid down in the Business Systems Plan (BSP). The following subtasks are activities relevant to this:

- Develop Profiles of the Existing Information Systems

This analysis produces flowcharts, matrices or other tables and diagrams of existing manual and computerized systems, business functions served, user departments involved, decision-making processes, and quantity and quality of service. This includes both internal and external information systems. Also the quantity, quality and cost of resources and facilities involved, e.g. hardware, software, personnel and skills, accommodation should be shown.

- Perform Data Review

This can take a number of forms, depending on the methodology in use and its underlying philosophy and assumptions [MADD83ISM], but in essence must establish the basic or fundamental data that the organization uses. One form which it might take is a high-level global data analysis exercise which would identify entities and relationships between entities. This would provide an outline corporate conceptual data model picture free of any organizational, hierarchical or implementation constraints.

The purpose of this task is to provide input for many of the other tasks in this phase. It is aimed at identifying the main overall types of information represented as data and their use in high-level terms, thereby enabling co-operating and integrated ISs to be planned jointly.

It will also serve as input to detailed data analysis activities, undertaken in later phases. The analysis task itself belongs to later projects, possibly partly in each of several IS developments.

- Perform Systems Audit

The systems audit task takes the results of the above tasks, evaluates the degree of success or failure, and identifies any particular requirements not currently being fulfilled. This is performed in terms of business needs and requirements rather than a technical evaluation.

2 Define Information Systems Objectives

In this task the team defines the objectives of:

- the totality of the information systems needed, i.e. to fit the BSP
- each existing information system. This may be an updating from previously stated objectives, e.g. to add that by certain future dates particular types of facilities and processes will be available to give particular types of information to particular groups of users.

The level at which these objectives are defined is at a lower level than those laid down by BSP but at a higher level than a set of technical objectives. This means that the objectives clearly reflect the requirements of BSP and are stated in terms of the business needs, but in addition include the functional and user objectives.

So, for example, where the BSP might state that sales of a particular group of products is a priority and that the sales force must be better informed about these products, the ISSP objectives might be to state in general what information should be available to the sales force, how this is expected to improve the sales and the general form in which the information should be available, e.g. the major points of recent research concerning the products to be available at the time of discussions with the clients. This clearly leaves the technical detail of whether the salesman is provided with a set of manuals, or a portable terminal connected to a research database, or anything else, out of the objectives at this stage.

3 Perform Technology Review

In the rapidly changing areas of information technology and methods it is important that new developments be reviewed and evaluated systematically. They should be reviewed as to their effectiveness in contributing towards the information systems objectives and their appropriateness for the organization. For example even if a particular development could significantly contribute to the achieving of the objectives it may not be appropriate because it conflicts with existing procedures and technology. Each new development or class of development should be reviewed and its potential stated in a position statement.

Changes in technology may affect both:

- **external** demand for the organization's business products, goods and services, e.g. new technologies may increase or decrease demand from customers, or may suggest how existing products should be changed
- **internal** methods both of production of goods and services and of methods of management, control, planning, forecasting and feedback.

This task, or part of it, may be needed in BSP.

4 List and Describe Alternative Strategies

The task is to define a number of alternative strategies which each seek to fulfil the objectives defined above. The strategies might vary considerably in their approaches, scale, costs, benefits, time-scales and risks. As an example one alternative strategy might be to localize all information on a regional basis while another may consider a very tightly controlled centralized approach. The alternatives between adaptation of existing systems to meet the requirements and a totally radical approach might be considered.

5 Define Selection Criteria

The appropriate selection criteria for deciding on the strategy should be agreed. This might weight very heavily the minimization of either disruption or cost, for example.

Rating of the priorities between computer projects can be a complex exercise. Allocation of priorities requires careful judgement of a number of factors, principal of which is the contribution the ISs will make to the business objectives (see [DUCC83] and [MATL82]).

6 Evaluate Alternative Strategies

The alternative strategies of task 4 should evaluated according to the criteria defined in 5. The quality of the evolution and its implied recommendable decision should also be evaluated.

Example

Decision Analyser and Processor (DAP) is a software package [DAP88]. The decision-making team agree a list of alternatives (e.g. six models of cars) and a list of criteria (e.g. price, acceleration, seating, comfort), and relative weights of each criterion. Each team member types in his or her (subjective) scores out of 100 for each model of car and for each criterion, forming a matrix. The matrices are combined using appropriate multiplications to give an overall matrix. The alternative with the lowest total, i.e. ranked poorest in the combined view, can be discarded and the calculations repeated. Further alternatives can gradually be discarded till the better of the best two is found.

7 Select Strategy

An appropriate strategy is selected either as a result of the evaluation performed in task 6, or for any other reason!

8 Define Migration Plan

The migration plan states how to move from what has been identified in task 1 above as the current position to where the organization wants to be, i.e. that identified in task 2 above, given the selected strategy of task 6. The migration plan involves the following activity to be done for each IS:

- Define each Component Information System

The information system's totality is divided into its major component parts, each such part being a separate information system. This division should ideally be made on the basis of convenient data groupings as identified in the strategic data model coupled with the functional requirements necessary to meet the business objectives. This should ensure the minimum system interaction, and where interaction is necessary it will be on a manageable scale. Each information system so defined will be part of the basis of the organization's future and so the divisions need to be very carefully chosen. In practice other criteria, such as organizational structure, business functions and technology, may also influence the division. The criteria used and the justification of the breakdown should be documented in the Component IS Report.

Once the structure of each information system is defined its Terms of Reference is produced. Each **IS terms of reference** (TOR) should include:

- the objectives and benefits of the system
- the scope of the system
- the criteria by which it is to be judged
- the development strategy
- the time-scales of developments
- the resources to be allocated, including manpower and finance; and any constraints that are to be applied, e.g. that existing hardware is to be used, and that certain specified parts are to remain manual - the structure of the development team
- the relative priority
- the organizational impact. The introduction of computerized systems into an organization and work places is not a simple process, it often has an effect on the environment and changes people's attitudes, skills and perceptions.

The user's perception of the work and its performance may change, necessitating changes to the information system itself. Another possibility is that the IS may be rejected by the users or their representatives. As far as possible such eventualities should be predicted by examining the impact of the IS and taking preventive measures. If it is realized that the IS will affect the behaviour and responsibility patterns in the organization then this problem must be addressed prior to its introduction. The solution is unlikely to be a simple one concerning technical design, but is more likely to require organizational change.

9 Define Overall Information Systems Standards

Some standards will need to be defined that should be applied to all information systems. Such standards facilitate the development and maintenance process, they improve communication between participants and conserve resources in general. Particularly they restrict the range of skills and expertise needed within the organization. However, although some standards are essential they can prove restrictive in a rapidly developing environment and can be inappropriate in some circumstances. Any such standards should have their justification documented along with any exceptions to their application.

The following policy areas may be appropriate for overall standards.

Hardware and Software Acquisition Policies

Hardware and software planning subdivides into:

- equipment to support business *functions*, needing usage planning
- equipment to support the *development* of ISs, including implementation, transition and maintenance.

An organization may have a uniform policy for all hardware and software acquisition or, more usually, it may have a policy allowing differing types of hardware and software in different ISs or areas of the organization. There might or might not be guidelines about

- different pieces of the same system from one or from several suppliers
- interchangeable pieces from different suppliers
- equipment for different systems from the same or different suppliers.

If an organization wishes to specify a uniform acquisition policy for all developments, then it is defined at this stage, for example only a particular manufacturer's hardware is to be purchased, or three tenders must always be evaluated. Some organizations have policies about whether to buy, rent or lease; or different such policies for different types of equipment. A policy on expected lifetimes, depreciation and funding of replacements is usually needed.

Thus, for example, it may be appropriate to purchase mainframe computers, owing to the maturity of the marketplace and familiarity with them. Distributed minis and communications hardware may be leased owing to imminent changes. A DBMS may be purchased. Data dictionary and query language packages may be leased. Office automation facilities may be used through a bureau until requirements become sufficiently understood.

- Skills acquisition policy

Owing to the shortage of skilled computer personnel and the pressures to reduce the backlog of applications, the issue of skills acquisition and retention is an important one. The long term policy will probably be to develop in-house skills and awareness. It should not be assumed that the only skills required are technical ones, the question of communication skills and user education should also be addressed (see [BAIL82], [TI821018], [D8001], [C821209], [HUGH80]).

- Development methods policy

The use of common analysis, design and programming methodologies enables more flexible use of staff and provides a more controlled development.

- Tools and techniques policy

For example a standard query language, data dictionary, prototyping system, application generator or evaluation technique may give benefit. But such standards may be too restrictive, e.g. one editor, programming language, compiler or DBMS.

- Data and process administration policy

Standards for documentation, definitions, deletions, insertions, authority, privacy, integrity, security and recovery might be appropriate.

- Design standards policy

User interfaces, data transmission and file access may be areas for possible standards. Communication and interfaces standards across equipment that is initially not connected may enable easier connection and save replacement when interconnection is needed.

- Quality control and audit procedures and policy

The procedures for quality control and audit of information systems should be specified and the policy should include that the requirements be incorporated into the development process.

10 Review ISSP

Once completed, the tasks and products of ISSP should be regularly reviewed and updated in the light of changing circumstances and lessons learnt. However, before changing major planning decisions the advantages and disadvantages, including the disruptive effect of the change, must be fully evaluated. There is a trade-off between updating plans in the light of new circumstances and the desire for stability. It is often tempting to rush into a new technology fully appreciating all its benefits but underestimating the drawbacks, particularly those concerning the new skills required and the effect of the new system in the workplace.

4.10 Major Products Description for ISSP

There is a close correspondence between the tasks and major products. As such, only a few details are given for each major product, since the descriptions can be derived from the corresponding tasks.

Reports and documents mentioned may not necessarily correspond to physical documents of the same format. The information may be expressed as working papers, letters, memos, minutes of meetings and company procedural notices; and may be held in an office product, a word processor, an index or a data dictionary.

Information system development plans

Each IS may have a separate plan. This will be a statement of:

- the objectives and functions of the information system and their correspondence to the business objectives
- relative priority and any weighting factors
- resources for use by the system, expressed in terms of manpower, finance, time, hardware and software: IS *development* and *functional use* may be separated
- direction on acquisition of resources, which may be separated similarly: this cross-refers to the hardware and software acquisition policy and plans
- management structure of the development teams
- nomination of actual personnel to the project, i.e. a list of names, specifying the responsibilities and authority of each person
- terms of reference (TOR).

New systems and systems to be improved might be described separately from other existing systems, including stating priorities.

Example

In an example of an organization manufacturing, marketing and selling consumer disposables this level of planning was carried out each year as part of a total organizational plan [CAPP84]. It covered a seven year period, the first five by quarters and the last two by year. Each resource was included.

The manager responsible for information systems planning and development had to produce a report for each resource for each project. The major resource was labour and for this he produced the time series for each level of skill, showing the number of people required for each project, by quarters for five years and by year for two further years.

From the levels of skill totals it was simple arithmetic to calculate the labour costs, as the standard cost of each level of skill, including the possible impact of rising salaries and wages, was estimated centrally within the organization as part of BSP.

Similar tables were produced for other resources, sub-totalled for each resource, project and time period. The specification of these sub-totals was changed according to the needs of top management, but were standard throughout the organization at any one time. The individual plans for each part of the organization were then integrated with forecast income showing, for example, how and when marketing costs were to be affected by the application of computing techniques, how much this application itself was to cost, and when these costs were to occur.

In order to produce viable and meaningful plans the managers had to examine carefully and in some detail what developments were to be planned, their scope, and when and how they would integrate with other functional areas within the organization. This was both a finance-driven and an ongoing exercise.

Because of the nature of the organization's products, the technology, and the environment within which the organization operates, these plans were changed frequently. But their existence and the preceding exercises that their development involved were valuable in both the short and medium term. The plans provided objectives, purpose and constraints; and hence an environment within which people could work freely.

The information flow diagram in Figure 4.3, showing as arrows the main information flows between the main business functions for this example organization, was used as a basis for its ISSP. For brevity we omit details of the information flows - what types of data and how often they happen.

Many other tables, lists and matrices can be developed, e.g. showing which data is used by whom for what purpose and process. This includes the structures and relationships between the various types of feedback, advice, recommendations, decisions, queries, messages, approvals, reports and accounts [KOVA82].

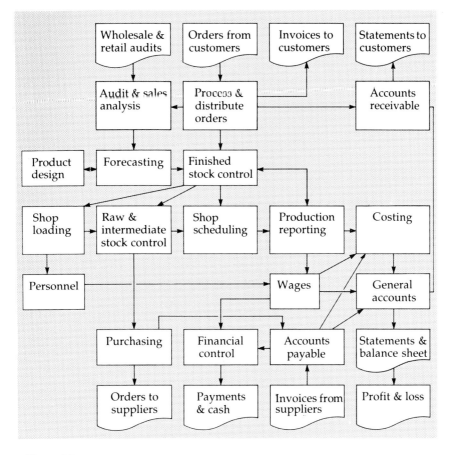

Figure 4.3

Impact of information systems on organizational structure

The development will affect the way people work. Thus new jobs may be created, some jobs may change, some people will need retraining. The organization's management structure may change. New methods of decision making may become available.

Hardware and software acquisition policy and plans

This states the acquisition policy and plans for all the information systems. There may be separate policies for each IS. As we explained earlier, there may also be different policies and plans for:

- business functions, i.e. usage
- development of the ISs.

65

Skills acquisition policy and plans

This states the policy and plans on skills similarly.

Development standards and practices

This should contain details of development standards and practices for IS developments. Tools and techniques should be included.

Data administration procedure report

In addition to specifying the procedures, this should contain details of the data administration function, specifying where this fits into the organization structure, the personnel that will manage it, their responsibilities and authority.

Quality control and auditing procedures report

This should state appropriate organization-wide procedures. Section 11.4 discusses this.

Considerations of possible applications of emerging technologies

This report should contain details of the technologies considered and how these may assist with the business functions.

Included should be details of:

- likely impact on the business function and organization structures
- perceived or estimated costs and benefits
- correspondence of the technologies to the long-term corporate strategy.

4.11 Resources for ISSP

The resources required will depend on the scale of planning. As intimated earlier, this will vary with the strategic importance of information systems. Also, the resources used will change with time and will relate to the nature of planning activity involved.

The work may be undertaken by a specialist in charge of planning corporate strategy, calling upon expertise in the many functions as appropriate.

Many large companies have a specialist planning function. By 1979, an estimated 45% of the Fortune 500 companies had to some extent adopted the state-of-the-art portfolio planning approach, first developed in the later 1970s. In 1983 there were 10 000 to 15 000 professional grade corporate planners in the UK [THAC83].

The resources required will depend on the size of the organization and the importance of ISs to meeting the business objectives. Some organizations, for example the banks, are more heavily committed to ISs than others. Generally, however, IS planning activities are under-resourced and often carried out in an ad hoc fashion as a reaction to events and problems.

Continuity between Business Strategic Planning (BSP) and ISSP is desirable and can best be achieved by ISSP being overseen by representatives from BSP. External resources, e.g. consultants, may also have a role to play. Certainly data-processing management and senior user management should also be involved. The exact composition of the investigating team will depend on the scope and scale of the work and the attitudes of user management.

4.12 Techniques and Tools for ISSP

The tools and techniques used will be particular to the planning activities and tasks. These may be proprietary or not.

It should be noted that many of the planning activities involve a great deal of communication which will take a variety of forms.

The following techniques may be appropriate for information gathering, communication and dissemination, including education and training:

- interviewing, structured and unstructured
- use of questionnaires
- group discussions
- presentations, oral and written briefings, walkthroughs.

The following are *some* of the tools and techniques that may be employed in modelling and analysis:

- BSP [IBMGE20-0527], BICS [KERN82], BMT [PEND82], Critical Success Factors [ROCK79], ISAC [LUND81]
- financial modelling techniques for evaluating costs and benefits, determination of priorities
- critical path analysis; Programme Evaluation and Review Technique (PERT); Resource Allocation and Multiple Project Scheduling (RAMPS)
- data dictionary system, for documentation, holding conceptual models and definitions

- expert system, for Decision Support and analysis.

[MADD83ISM] gives details for certain methodologies.

Representation on paper of relationships such as between business functions, organizational areas, information systems and requirements may be a problem. One possibility is to summarize the picture as a corporate information requirements matrix [KOVA74]. This is a table with, say, relevant business functions as headings to the columns and main information types, user departments or information systems to the left of the rows. The entries show:

- where decisions are made, where recommended and where confirmed
- problem areas, issues needing study
- information flows, feedback, advice, capture of information
- new requirements
- existing IS facilities.

Another possibility is to show departments both as the rows and as the columns, with entries showing the main information flows.

Sadly, established techniques and tools for ISSP are lacking, but some of the references contain suggestions particular to their individual authors.

4.13 General Comments on ISSP

This section has been used for:

- giving supporting arguments for some of the tasks - e.g. why plan?
- providing a perspective to the phase, and expressing ideas that do not fit elsewhere into our document structure.

It is worth repeating that the ISSP functions described in this chapter will not be appropriate for every type of organization, regardless of size. Nor is ISSP a uniform activity. These two factors must be borne in mind when considering ISSP.

Why plan?

The purpose of ISP is to plan for future developments which are outlined through the strategic planning process, so that they take place in accordance with the strategy and not by default.

In many organizations, parallel developments take place wherein there is little sharing of knowledge, expertise, skills and tools. A certain amount of reinvention takes place. The same mistakes are repeated.

68

The *purpose* of planning includes to identify the commonality between various developments and to use a single set of tools and techniques, make effective use of skills and resources, and build upon the systems already in place or available. It therefore takes the form of software engineering - reusing components of other systems; repeating the development tasks without undergoing a process of reinvention.

As technology changes, planning becomes important to avoid proliferation of incompatible systems and all the consequences which ensue from such development.

Planning Information System Functional Usage

Thus far in our treatment and discussion of the information system development (ISD) process, we have tended to take a very restricted view, perhaps based on assumptions which do not correspond to the reality of ISD.

Briefly, we have restricted our perspective to the technical issues of ISD. While this perspective is appropriate when considering the latter phases, the *context* in which these must be considered has been too narrow.

In particular, we have given no consideration to the impact ISs have on the users' methods of working and other organizational issues, nor to the impact of new development tools and techniques on ISD. There is a parallel between these two issues.

Consider the usage of new tools and techniques. The first observation to be made is that the introduction of new practices for ISD is seldom without *conflict*. This can happen even though you might expect computer professionals to be professional!

The second point to note is that use of the aforementioned tools and techniques *changes the manner of ISD*. Reflect on the use of query languages, user-friendly operating systems, program-generators, analysis and design methodologies.

The point being made is that, even for a receptive and technically knowledgeable community, *a significant amount of planning is necessary* to ensure that the use of new tools and techniques will be successful.

It has been stressed that each IS is developed to serve particular business needs, even though a computer professional's concern is mainly with the technical aspects of system development. The developed information systems, like the tools that are used by the developers, have to be *'introduced'* into the user's work environment. They have the effect of *changing this environment* in the first instance. After a certain amount of use, the user's perception of how the work is to be performed changes, and therefore results in *continual modifications* to the IS.

These two aspects are very significant and people ignore them at severe costs. The role of organizational functional IS usage planning cannot be over-stressed.

To further the realization of these points, certain assumptions that some people may hold about ISD must be dispelled. We assume, rightly or wrongly, that computerized information systems are in the main automated versions of their manual predecessors. Although the new systems may perform the same end-functions as their predecessors, the main purpose of their development is to change the work organization and processing. This will impact the job design, responsibilities and authority of the affected individuals, while altering the organizational behaviour and management mechanisms.

Some people naively assume a commonality of organizational purpose. [KEEN81] states: 'Most studies of complex decisions suggest that companies are far more pluralistic than we conveniently assume. Pettigrew's analysis of a decision to purchase a computer, for example, reveals innumerable territorial disputes, manoeuvring for position, conflict over goals and *irreconcilable differences* in perspective amongst organizational units. Believers in pluralism do not find that surprising but most computer specialists do. ... The key point is that designers must recognize that far from being divorced from the messy "politics", information technology has a major impact on a critical resource and source of power.' In the context of planning information system functional usage, it is worth examining the opportunities for changing the organizational structure. Organization structures reflect the manner in which work is organized and processed. Despite automation of many operations, the same organization structures persist. They may beneficially be changed in line with the changes in work organization and processing, resulting from the impact of IS.

[JONE83] examines office automation by questioning the organization of the office. For example word processing has had a major impact. A previous structure from pre-word-processing days may be no longer appropriate.

Planning Information System Development

In most organizations engaged in in-house development of applications, a variety of software systems are used. For organizations with relatively little information system development, it is relatively easy to control and utilize a small number of software packages each with simple and separate functionality, whether externally or internally developed.

70

Namely, there is a lack of integrated use of software tools and techniques. Some organizations have taken steps to share and integrate data amongst different information systems and we now see the rationalization and integration of data definitions, via the use of data dictionaries. However, the widespread sharing of tools, techniques and practices has yet to materialize.

While some computer professionals have just woken to the possibilities of prototyping, engineers have been engaged in it for over fifty years. The same applies to the use of graphics, pictures and images in conveying information. Computerized tools for those techniques have not been available until recently. Certain types of organizations therefore have people with skills in techniques that are new to some computer professionals.

Information systems, tools and techniques are often used in ways not imagined by their designers. For example, text editors have been used for word processing, for design of screen layouts, for simulation of screen-based interactive systems and as simple file query systems. Financial packages have been used in many non-financial areas, like the use of VISICALC in designing a plumbing system and in project management.

Available software can be imaginatively used, without the extra costs of acquiring a variety of similar function software, through *planned development*. This entails identifying the requirements for tools and techniques across a broad range and matching with the facilities and features of available hardware and software. The same applies to the effective use of skills and expertise, e.g. engineers with CAD/CAM experience may be suitable to advise on the design of business information systems using graphics; corporate communications personnel could advise on how to determine the impact of ISs; advertising consultants could advise on the design of interfaces for easy-to-use systems.

4.14 References and Sources

Despite the size of this chapter, we have not made full use of the material in the various references. We cannot encompass the breadth of ideas and issues relating to ISSP. Specialists may find reading some of the references interesting though the list is not comprehensive. As yet, we have not come across a taxonomy of the tools and techniques that may be used in ISSP. Many of the references contain techniques used by their authors but these are mostly not widely adopted and cannot be usefully referred to. Nor may they be applicable in every circumstance.

Not all these references have been cited. Appendix 3 gives further references.

BAIL82: Lotte Bailyn. Career Fulfilment Strategies for Mature Engineers. *Computer Design* (Oct 1982) p73-76.

BUSS83: M.D.J. Buss. How to rank computer projects. *Harvard Business Review* (Jan-Feb 1983) pp118-125.

CAPP84: L. Capper sent R.N. Maddison a draft of this example in 1984. This example has also been developed in P792: *Information Systems and IT for Managers*, Blocks 2 and 3. The Open University (1988).

C821209: Changing attitudes of staff. *Computing* (9 Dec 1982).

CW830310: *Computer Weekly* Mar 10 1983, p21. The article is on the impact of MAPPER on IS design and IS on work management.

D8001: Dwindling supply of people. *Datamation* (Jan 1980) pp82 and 85.

DAP88: Decision Analyser and Processor. C. Champion & M. LaCosta. ITT (BS) Ltd. (Tel: 01 607 6730). A.I. Kovacs demonstrated this to R.N. Maddison.

HUGH80: J. Hughes. The management teaching gap. *Management Today* (May 1980) pp109-112.

IBMGE20-0527: *Business Systems Planning - Information Systems Planning Guide*. GE20-0527. IBM Corp.

JONE83: F. Jones. The Question of Inter-connection. *Computer Management* (Jan and Feb 1983).

KEEN81: P.G.W. Keen. Information Systems and Organizational Change. *Comms. of the ACM*, Vol 24, No 1 (Jan 1981) pp24-33. Also see a review of the article in 'Computing Reviews', (Nov 1982) p496.

KERN82: D.V. Kerner. Introduction to Business Information Control Study Methodology (BICS). In [MATL82].

KOVA74: A.I. Kovacs. Information Systems for Project Management. INTERNET Congress in International Project Management. Paris (1974).

KOVA82: A.I. Kovacs. The Electronic Office - A Guide for the O.R. Practitioner. An Operational Model for Information System and Management Structure Design. Presentation at London Business School (31 March 1982).

LUND81: M. Lundeberg, G. Goldkuhl and A. Nilsson. *Information System Development: A Systematic Approach*. Prentice-Hall (1981).

MADD83ISM: R.N. Maddison, G.J. Baker, L. Bhabuta, G. Fitzgerald, K. Hindle, J.H.T. Song, N. Stokes, J.R.G. Wood. *Information System Methodologies*. Wiley Heyden on behalf of the British Computer Society (1983) 130pp. ISBN 0 471 90332 9.

MATL82: G.L. Matlin. What is the value of investment in information systems. In *Economics of Information Processing* Vol 1. Eds: R. Goldberg and H. Lorin. John Wiley and Sons (1982) ISBN 0-471-09206-1.

MCFA83: F.W. McFarlan, J.L. McKenney and P. Pyburn. The information archipelago - plotting a course. *Harvard Business Review* (Jan-Feb 1983) pp145-156.

MCLE82: J. Hagwood Ed. *Evolutionary Information Systems*. North-Holland Publishing Co. (1982). Quote by Prof. E.F. McLean on pp251.

MUMF82: E. Mumford and D. Henshall. Review of book: 'A participative approach to computer system design. Halstead Press, New York (1979)'. In *Computing Reviews* (Feb 1982).

PEND82: A.D. Pendleton. 'BMT': A Business Modelling Technology. In [MATL82].

ROCK79: J.F. Rockart. Critical Success Factors. *Harvard Business Review* (Mar-Apr 1979) pp81-91.

THAC83: J. Thackray. America's Stunted Planning. *Management Today* (Mar 1983) pp88-94.

TI821018: Are Whizzes Washed Up at 35? *Time* (Oct 18 1982) p58.

4.16 Ideas and Suggestions

- Assess the SWOT of the main IS services, products, and costs in your organization.

- Assess to what extent the top management included people with the right knowledge and skills in ISs and IT.

- Assess to what extent the top management really understands the potentials of ISs.

- Assess how well the top Management Services, IS services, DP managers and/or Information Officer really understand the potential of ISs for the organization's benefit.

- To what extent can the management rely on IS and IT staff?

- How does the organization quantify and measure IS efficiency, benefits and performance?

- How, as a long-term average, has IS costs relevant to your area fallen in real terms or its products and services improved for no increase in costs? Will the trends continue?

5 INFORMATION SYSTEM TACTICAL PLANNING

5.1 Introduction

The ISSP introduction should be borne in mind when reading this chapter. By information system tactical planning (ISTP) we mean the planning for one information system (IS).

What some people regard as a group of related information sub-systems we may regard as one IS for the purpose of reading this chapter. In general a logical database contains many types of data organized so that all users' requirements can be satisfied. The data types are used for many applications. Each application may have one or more logical views of some of the data types and may have one or more application programs or a query language facility. Each application program or query process usually provides facilities for many types of end-user transactions. Many-end-users may make transactions concurrently. All this is certainly within one IS.

To us each organization uses many information systems. Each IS includes many applications, or sub-systems. Each IS needs ISTP. For example a Sales Order Processing IS may include as applications or sub-systems:

- customer entry
- order entry
- invoicing, i.e. billing
- despatch, i.e. shipping.

These share information, but apply it in different ways.

But we would also regard as one IS a system with many related logical databases, for example one per borough where many boroughs' data are all serviced on the same suite of mainframe computers, each borough having the same types of requirements and applications, e.g. rates. There may be a separate IS for say planning applications for the same boroughs, and another IS for finance. Each IS will have security facilities, so for example rates staff in one borough office can only make certain transactions and only access the relevant data occurrences for their own borough.

The trends are that initially separate ISs grow, have interfaces added to allow flow of information between them, and then perhaps eventually merge.

5.2 Framework Diagram for ISTP

Figure 5.1 illustrates the planning and other phases for the current state of one organization that has five information systems with various structures of their phases as described below.

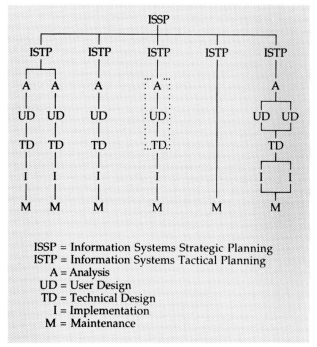

ISSP = Information Systems Strategic Planning
ISTP = Information Systems Tactical Planning
A = Analysis
UD = User Design
TD = Technical Design
I = Implementation
M = Maintenance

Figure 5.1

From left to right the five information systems illustrate:

• an IS with two applications or groups of applications, or two subsystems

• an IS with one application

• an IS with three phases performed together, e.g. using prototyping

• an IS in its maintenance phase when the planning is being done

• an IS regarded by end-users as two separate systems, though related and so analysed and technically designed together as two applications or sub-systems.

The three phases within the dotted box form a project with its ISPP. The IS in its maintenance phase has no ISPP. Otherwise each column has ISPP for each phase, as described in Chapter 6.

Each IS has management, and possibly data administration, associated with it. The totality also has associated management and data administration.

For *each* ISTP in Figure 5.1 the tasks for that ISTP team are as shown in Figure 5.2.

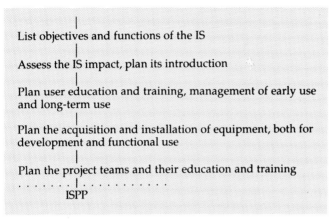

List objectives and functions of the IS

Assess the IS impact, plan its introduction

Plan user education and training, management of early use and long-term use

Plan the acquisition and installation of equipment, both for development and functional use

Plan the project teams and their education and training

ISPP

Figure 5.2

These tasks are expanded in Sections 5.7 and 5.9.

5.3 Definition of ISTP

The purpose of ISTP is to translate the IS strategic plans for a particular IS into effective action plans. This planning is at the individual information system level. The structure of the next level down is determined, i.e. what application or applications exist and what are their terms of reference.

In addition there may be more detailed planning at the individual phase level, e.g. the planning of the analysis phase. Planning that involves determining policies, constraints, resources and directions may or may not exist at the phase, task and activity level.

5.4 Objectives of ISTP

After the ISTP for a particular information system has been completed:

- long-term, medium-term and short-term plans for both the various developments and all types of business functional use of this information system will have been drawn up, agreed and approved by all concerned
- plans for the various developments will be specified as projects and phases, with agreed schedules and resources
- appropriate standards will be agreed, if not already agreed in ISSP
- methods of coordination, review, control and feedback across projects and phases will be agreed, if not already agreed in ISSP
- planning products such as documents needed for project planning will be available.

5.5 Scope of ISTP

Each ISTP covers all aspects of its particular information system. This includes:

- coordination with other information systems
- liaison with users or their representatives
- methods of project planning
- methods of feedback, review and control
- the analysis and subdivision of developments into projects and phases
- methods of management of functional use
- resources and schedules.

5.6 Prerequisites of ISTP

The following ISTP prerequisites for a particular IS should have been produced at ISSP:

- statement of the information system priorities
- statement on the range of technology to be used
- statement of guidelines to be followed and any particular considerations, e.g. hardware and software acquisition policy; use of state-of-art technology; data is to be transmitted on the public network; and so on
- component IS report

- TOR for this IS component, including overall business objectives and functions for this IS
- statement of ISs standards
- appropriate policy papers and position papers.

5.7 Task List for ISTP

The order here does not imply the action sequence. The tasks for a particular information system development may form part of a Programme Evaluation and Review Technique (PERT) network or Critical Path Network (CPN) for the IS development.

This task list includes some tasks which for a particular IS development may belong at a lower planning level; e.g. planning for a particular phase such as Analysis or User Design or for a task or an activity within such a phase.

These tasks apply to one particular information system or to each group of related information systems or sub-systems - e.g. with part parallel development.

1   Produce a detailed statement of the objectives and functions of the IS being planned.

2   Assess the impact of this IS on the business functions and on the organization.

3   Plan this information system's introduction into the user environment.

4   Plan *end-user* education and training for this IS.

5   Plan the management of the initial usage of this IS.

6   Plan for flexibility, e.g. how the IS will have features allowing easy modification, e.g. as a result of experience of its use.

7   Plan the mature usage of this IS, i.e. after the IS is no longer young.

8   Plan the hardware, computer power, storage capacity and telecommunications for this IS, and buildings or accommodation.

9   Plan hardware and software acquisition and installation for this IS.

10   Plan the education and training of the development staff for this IS.

11   Plan the structure of the project teams for this IS.

12   Produce or update from ISSP products into greater detail:
- IS cost and benefit analysis report
- Global data analysis report for this IS.

5.8 Major Products List for ISTP

Any of the following may be omitted if not appropriate. These apply to each IS.

- more detailed statement of this IS objectives and functions
- information system introduction plan
- information system modification plan
- IS cost and benefit analysis report, with a retrospective report comparing the past plans, costs, benefits, impact, and success or failure of this IS
- education and training policy and plans report
- global data analysis report
- list of membership of each project team and TOR of each project within this IS.

5.9 Task Descriptions for ISTP

1 Produce a more detailed statement of the objectives and functions of the system being planned

- specify the correspondence to the business objectives and functions
- specify the category of users within the business function i.e. areas; departments, divisions, sections, groups; locations; class of personnel - technical staff, supervisors, lower-level managers
- specify the operational criteria - this states the operational capability of the system, e.g.: must be fault tolerant; low reliability acceptable; acceptable mean time between failures
- specify the degree of extensibility, e.g. unlikely to be extended; complete change possible
- specify backward and forward compatibility, e.g. it must be capable of operating on existing file structures; or it must fit into the design strategy of the IS being planned for the future; or it is a one-off and no compatibility is needed
- specify sideways compatibility, e.g. availability of interfaces to other systems.

Example

An example of an abridged draft working paper within this task follows.

'Develop and provide an IS which enables specified middle managers to access operational control data of their respective business functions with an easy-to-use enquiry system.

Hard copy output is desirable.

The business functions for which this system is required are as follows...

The following subject databases are expected to be accessed... The system should be capable of accommodating further subject databases. These databases are currently centrally located but the plans to distribute these in line with the further localized development of remote sites imply...

The desirable features, facilities and interfaces...'

2 Assess the impact of the information system on the business functions

Information systems have an impact on the business functions. The scale of the impact will depend on the nature of the IS and the environment in which it operates.

This task relates to planning the usage of an information system. Each information system should be designed for serving particular business requirements. Its use may not be as automatic as may be assumed.

Examples of the impact include changes in the work organization and processing, resulting in reduction of staff for the particular function or the same staff providing a substantial improved service. Decision-making processes may change. For employees, this may mean re-training, redundancy, job changes or relocation. For the organization, this means changes in the organization's structure (static), and the operating structure (dynamic). It also affects the operating costs and the competitive position of the organization.

The following aspects should be considered in assessing the impact of IS:
- changes in operating costs of the business function/unit
- changes in the management structure of the organization
- changes in the lines of communication
- changes in job design, responsibility, authority and scope
- changes in work organization and management.

3 Plan the information system's introduction into the user environment

The need to plan the 'introduction' arises out of the following observations in addition to the issues raised in the preceding task.

Only relatively few end-user representatives are likely to be involved with the analysts and designers in the development of an IS. Relatively many will first meet the IS after implementation.

Interaction with IS is likely to be interactive, i.e. from a workstation or terminal. If not already in place, these will require installation and appropriate connections.

Changes in job design, work organization and management structures usually occur gradually. These changes need to be introduced and managed in accordance with the effect of the information systems, with adequate thought, discussion and allowance for human factors.

4 Plan end-user education and training for this IS

This includes:

- Brief staff on the business objectives and the correspondence of the IS to these objectives.
- Brief users on the purpose and functionality of the IS. Educate on the technology being used, if appropriate.
- Advise users on communication and liaison with the development staff. Users need to communicate their requirements effectively to the designers. According to Prof. McLean [MCLE82] 'Even when designers think they are user-oriented, the results come out the same old way. A study by Gringras at UCLA of the designer's concept of the user and the user's self-concept, using Osgood's Semantic Differential Instrument, showed these to be very different. *But the users understood the designers much better*. The designer's concept of the 'ideal user' was very like their self-concept!'

5 Plan the management of the initial usage of this information system

This task is planning for the period immediately after the introduction of the IS. It is concerned with devising arrangements for monitoring the behaviour of the IS, and reviewing and controlling the IS. That expands into:

- monitor the costs and benefits against those predicted
- monitor the organizational impact against that predicted
- what are the deficiencies?
- what lessons are to be learnt?
- what changes are necessary?
- what are the most and least attractive features of the system as perceived by the users?

This task occurs once for each change to the IS that is non-trivial from the users' viewpoint.

6 Plan for flexibility, e.g. features for modification

An IS invariably undergoes changes over time. The initial changes may result from incorrect implementation of requirements. More fundamental changes may arise in response to informal information flows filling the organizational and behavioural gaps in the system provided. A mature use of the IS may develop as a result of changes that are required to deal with unanticipated effects of the IS. The IS functions and thus the business functions change through the direct and indirect impact of the IS.

7 Plan the mature use of this IS

This task is concerned with rationalization of IS usage. Experience with information systems and technology now enables effective control mechanisms to be built so that near-optimum utilization is achieved. Also, widespread transfer of technology may take place [MCFA83 Phases 3 and 4 on pp148, 149].

8 Plan the hardware, computer power, storage capacity, and communications

This is concerned with determining the hardware requirements to support the projected workload. The following aspects may be considered:

- computing power requirements
- data storage requirements
- telecommunications capacity requirements
- terminals and workstations
- response times
- reliability, up time, servicing, maintenance, testing
- special arrangements to cope with peaks in demand
- buildings, accommodation.

9 Plan hardware and software acquisition and installation

This will be in accordance with the acquisition policy. It will entail:

- bench marking
- demonstrations
- tendering

- planning the installation of the hardware
- planning the installation of software
- logistics planning.

10 Plan the education and training of the development staff for this IS

This involves:

- brief on business objectives and functions
- training in communication skills, interviewing, questionnaires
- specialist and technical training
    - programming languages, DBMS, utilities, standards, and so on
    - tools and techniques
    - project management practices
    - methodology.

11 Plan this IS project teams' structures

Project team structures need not be uniform but should reflect the nature of the information systems being developed and the technology being used, also taking into account the priorities and business needs.

The task is concerned with planning the team structures, so as to make optimum use of available skill and expertise, e.g. use of engineers familiar with computer-aided design in the design of graphic displays.

Requirements for quality control and auditing should be considered in ascertaining whether to involve specialists in these functions directly in the development of the IS.

5.10 Major Product Descriptions for ISTP

The comments at the start of Section 4.10 for ISSP major product descriptions also apply here.

Information System Objectives and Functions

This was described and an example given in the task description in Section 5.9.

Information System Introduction Plan

Each IS may have a separate plan that specifies how the system is to be introduced into the users' environment. There may be separate plans for each area.

Information System Modifications Plan

Each IS may have a separate plan that specifies modifications to the IS features and functions. Where these modifications affect other information systems, the modifications may be specified collectively.

IS Cost and Benefit Analysis Report

This report is likely to be updated incrementally. The initial version should contain details of the assumptions on which the cost and benefit analysis is based.

During the course of system development and following implementation, these assumptions and predictions will probably change slightly.

The report should specify both the tangible and the non-tangible costs and benefits.

Education and Training Policy and Plans

This document specifies the training policy and plans for both the users of the IS and the developers of IS.

Global Data Analysis Report

It should contain results of the global data analysis exercise. These may be held in a data dictionary.

The scope of the data analysis activity undertaken must be specified together with details of the methods and methodology or conventions used. It may additionally contain pointers to further exercises of this kind.

Retrospective Information System Cost and Benefit, Impact and Success Report

This corresponds to a number of tasks. Its content should include information that will aid in the formulation of future strategy and development policies. This includes reviewing past plans and estimated costs and benefits, noting the impact, success or failure, and deducing what changes of plans are consequently needed.

5.11 Resources

The details in Section 4.11 also apply here.

5.12 Techniques and Tools

The details in Section 4.12 also apply here.

5.13 General Comments

A number of IS technologies, e.g. for different types of information systems, may be in use in an organization. The nature of planning activities as described in terms of the three categories of planning, ISSP, ISTP and ISPP, will vary for different types of information systems.

An information system as considered here may be thought of as comprising a number of computer applications or related sub-systems, which collectively serve one or more business functions and use one or more IS technologies of the kind described in the framework diagrams.

The development of an information system may be:

• incremental, i.e. staggered, one or more sub-systems developed and implemented concurrently, then some more applications and features added, and so on

• developed in parallel, i.e. parallel development of component sub-systems

• based on a particular methodology or a combination of such

• based on some new collection of principles.

Such decisions about which approach is to be used may vary from one IS to another within the organization: each decision then belongs to the ISTP. Alternatively there may be an organization-wide policy in ISSP, as noted in Chapter 4.

Whichever approach is taken, the function of the ISSP phase includes undertaking detailed localized planning of those aspects that are common to all ISs. ISTP should cover detailed localized planning of aspects common to the various component sub-systems.

Example

Figure 5.3 illustrates scheduling ISTP. Time runs across the diagram.

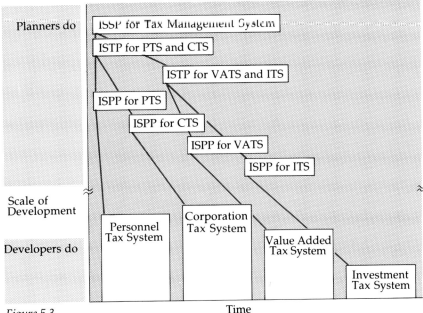

Figure 5.3

This example Tax Management information system has the following component sub-systems:

- Corporation Tax System (CTS)
- Personnel Tax System (PTS)
- Value Added Tax System (VATS)
- Investment Tax System (ITS)
- Tax Procedures and Guidance System (TPGS).

Assume that the development of these sub-systems is staggered. Also assume that the Personal Tax System and the Corporation Tax System were planned together and developed first. Then, after some development period, the above kind of picture will emerge. The last sub-system, TPGS, has not yet been scheduled and is omitted from the diagram.

The purpose of the example and the diagram is to illustrate the relationship of ISTP to ISPP particularly regarding scheduling. For simplicity we have drawn the developments as though they were done sequentially: in practice they would overlap.

87

5.14 References and Sources

Three of the references in Section 4.14 apply here, e.g. [MADD831SM, MCFA83, MCLE82].

5.16 Ideas and Suggestions

- Apply the ideas and suggestions in 3.16 and 4.16 to a single IS in your area of your organization, or to those of its facilities that are relevant to you, or to suggestions and plans for its change and evolution.
- Can people cope with all the complexity, features and facilities?
- Does everyone use the system, or are some people afraid?
- Does everyone understand and use all the features and facilities?
- Can the IS developers and providers keep up with and produce everything that people ask for as improvements?

6 INFORMATION SYSTEM PROJECT PLANNING

6.1 Introduction

Increasing concern has been expressed in recent years over the difficulties in meeting deadlines for information system and computer projects. Over the same period, however, anxiety over staff recruitment has decreased, indicating that lack of resources was not the prime reason for the failure to meet target dates. It would appear, therefore, that the problem lies more with the productivity and experience of existing computer staff, and in particular with the dearth of people able to estimate, plan and control projects well. It has now reached the stage in some organizations where failure is accepted as normal and where projects that incur a 'small' delay of three to twelve months are considered as major achievements. One contributory factor in this has been the assumption by general management that the control of a systems development project is the sole preserve of the computer expert. This mistaken assumption may in turn lead to:

- the delegation of management responsibility becoming abdication of it
- the belief that computer staff have the knowledge, training and ability to manage their own skills.

Deficiencies in the area of project management arise because:

- many data-processing practitioners have not been trained in the planning and control of time and resources
- they lack the support of experienced managers
- commonly accepted professional disciplines in other fields are not fully used
- the kind of training provided to practitioners tends to concentrate on technical specialization, e.g. hardware or particular software
- they are expected to learn many skills 'on the job'
- their selection and evaluation tends to look more at their technical skills and experience than at their project management and interpersonal skills.

Organizations which have a major commitment to computing may take the trouble to construct staff training programmes which develop general management skills, but this is still not common practice.

6.2 General Principles

Project management is concerned with both:

- the planning and internal review and control of project tasks and activities

- relating the individual project to the overall objectives of the organization. Many of the techniques used in the planning and control of system development would be familiar to engineers, architects and other professionals who frequently need to co-ordinate a diverse set of activities.

In system development there is an extremely close relationship between the notion of a system 'life-cycle' and the management of the development task. Whether the phases of the development life-cycle are considered as separate entities or regarded as stages in the whole project, the principles of planning and control which should be applied remain the same. The general approach to project management can be described under the following headings:

- the analysis of the project into the jobs to be done

- estimation of the work content of these jobs

- planning the work and allocating resources

- controlling performance and reporting progress

- controlling change.

Since project planning involves thinking and deciding about these activities in advance of action, we have included all these together in this chapter rather than for example putting project management in Chapter 2 before the planning leading to it had been explained, or for example leaving the planning of controlling performance and change till Chapter 11.

6.3 Analysing the Project

Project management is based to a large extent on the decomposition of complex tasks into smaller ones which, it is hoped, are then easier to resolve. This decomposition is usually based on a simple hierarchy of definitions such that a project consists of a number of stages, each stage requires a number of tasks to take place, and each task will comprise a number of activities. Hence:

- a **stage** will normally coincide with one of the phases identified within the system life-cycle

- a **task** is a group of related activities under the control of one person

- an **activity** is a specific job within a task: it will usually be performed by one person.

In each of the previous definitions for each action:

- there should be a clear start and finish point, i.e. **events**
- the **duration** of work-content should be prescribed in advance
- the completion of the work should be signalled by an identifiable **end-product**, e.g. the completion of an activity will be marked by a project **milestone**.

Thus it should be possible to have a standard hierarchical framework of phases, tasks and activities whatever the nature of the computer application. This should serve as an effective communication basis between planners, managers, IS specialists, developers, users and anyone else involved. Computer packages can provide substantial benefits in project management.

6.4 Estimating the Work Content of Jobs

Identifying the jobs to be done is considered to be a necessary prerequisite to the more difficult task of estimating the amount of work or time required to carry out each job.

Estimating can be based on one or more foundations:

- past experience of development performance
- the personal competence of the estimator
- accumulated experience and information on certain key parameters
- established industry standards.

Although there are often a number of qualitative factors associated with certain areas of system development work, it is possible to approach the task of estimating in a methodical way:

- make a broad estimate for each stage, task and activity based on the judgement and experience of the estimator
- estimate the work content for each activity
- having estimated each activity, accumulate a total for each task and compare it with the broad estimate made initially for that task
- arrive at a total of task estimates for the stage by accumulating the totals for all tasks
- add to this grand total allowances for project management, direct supervision and a contingency factor to provide for unforeseen events or delays.

It may be advisable or necessary to formalize the estimating process through documentation and a standard estimating procedure.

6.5 Planning the Work and Allocating Resources

Having identified activities and tasks, and estimated their work content, the next stage is concerned with matching these jobs and the work they represent to the resources available. Ideally, these resources should be known and should be available for commitment to the project on a full-time basis. In practice, however, the project manager may find that the estimated total manpower requirement cannot be met from existing resources within the agreed time-scale, or that the need for certain special skills will require some training or even recruitment during the project.

Plans can be represented in a number of different ways ranging in their degree of complexity from elaborate networks to simple Gantt or bar charts. In practice it often happens that the more sophisticated approaches are the most useful for the initial identification of activities and drawing up of the plan, whereas the simpler techniques are much more effective for the review and control of the plan when it is put into effect.

Ultimately, planning is a mechanism for identifying what has to be done and the means of anticipating problems. Plans should not be regarded as fixed and inviolable, with people being reluctant to change them. Rather plans should be subject to regular review, although not necessarily to frequent change. The existence of such a plan provides the knowledge with which to respond to factors affecting the project, in order to minimize their adverse effect. Without a plan there is a danger that actions will be taken which are wrong in themselves or would have a knock-on effect on subsequent activities.

6.6 Controlling Performance and Reporting Progress

In the past, the control of projects was typified by the response 'my program is 90% complete'. Performance of an imprecise task set by the supervisor would be assessed subjectively by the programmer and accepted at face value. There are, unfortunately, many management services, information and data processing departments which still operate in this fashion and in which staff are not trained in more precise methods of the control of progress. Problems tend to arise in such a situation not only because the assessment of progress is in error but also because the amount of time left to resolve the problem is minimal.

Effective control is generally achieved by planning the work in detail, allocating it in amounts that are achievable within set periods of time, and through the specification of how the achievement will be measured. Thus there must be some concrete evidence of achievement such as a report, document or set number of lines of code. The project manager will therefore know which activities are planned for the next three to four months and, within each task, will know the activities that have to be completed and the resources that have been allocated. The project manager will want to maintain control of the work on a weekly basis whilst providing management and user feedback on, say, a monthly basis. A variety of techniques are available for achieving such control and they can be classified broadly under the headings of:

- short-term scheduling
- progress monitoring
- project reporting.

6.7 Control of Changes

It is an inevitable feature of system development that users and management, for a variety of reasons, change their minds and discover new requirements which need to be incorporated at some stage into the system design. From the point of view of project control there are usually three disciplines recommended for responding to requests for change:

- to agree a period when the system design is 'frozen' and changes can not be considered until the 'frozen' specification has been implemented
- to ensure that some formal mechanism exists for authorizing and processing changes after the system has been officially 'signed-off' by the user
- to ensure that any changes that are not accepted are recorded for the next formal review of the system in operation.

Excessive change that might call into question the quality of the systems analysis work may create a situation in which the project has to be re-evaluated in the light of the new requirements.

6.8 A Prerequisite Balance in Management

We found that some of the management and control topics apply throughout the framework. It has been explicitly or implicitly stated that some principles of good management and administration must apply to construction of information systems, as it does on the factory floor, the supermarket, the sales office, the production platform, the accounts office and the warehouse.

1   Someone must have authority and the commensurate responsibility for the job.

2   The person given responsibility must be granted adequate staff.

3   The staff should operate in a synergetic environment, where widespread experience and sound theory can be melded.

4   Staff should be partially drawn from the industry for whom the system is done and from several levels, trained and re-trained.

5   Communication amongst staff and users must be open at several levels.

6   Planning should exist before, during and after the system is constructed, be consistent and be subject to controls.

7   Controls should be planned and be active enough to provide the reports on activities.

8   Feasibility of continuance and completion of the whole project and its parts should be considered in advance and reviewed whenever appropriate during the project.

9   Sound objectives should be stated, tested, restated or modified with agreement.

10   A sound financial case should be made, as it is for all corporate projects.

11   Success requires good documentation.

12   Independent reviews should be periodically staged by various groups including auditors, committees and users.

13   Prejudice against and preference for one segment being implemented ought to be periodically examined at the highest level.

14   Influences from internal politics must be recognized, but as far as possible kept out of the way of the IS development project teams.

Some readers may be disappointed to find this reminder, as it is not exclusively applicable to information systems. Other readers will be disappointed that the reminder is not advocated as a prerequisite to success. The secret may indeed be yet to be discovered, but it is suspected that a proper approach is to take all into account and balance them properly. Excess of one is as bad as absence of another.

6.9 Summary

Many computer staff who become project leaders are not only light on supervisory experience within their own functional area but also will rarely have had exposure to the management of multi-resourced teams and the responsibility for performance to an external customer when involved with large projects.

The aim of this chapter, therefore, has been to describe some general principles applicable to the planning of computer projects. The following minimum requirements should be set for all projects irrespective of their size and nature. These should serve as a useful foundation from which to build up a comprehensive and effective set of project management standards:

- ensure that the terms of reference and objectives for the project are clearly stated and understood
- ensure that the person appointed to manage a project has the requisite personal skills and access to the resources necessary to fulfil commitments
- ensure that adequate procedures exist and are used to:
  - analyse the jobs that have to be done
  - estimate the resources required
  - plan and allocate the work
  - control performance.

- ensure that satisfactory arrangements are introduced to achieve user participation and effective management control of the project.

6.16 Ideas and Suggestions

- To what extent might joint industry and university liaison and projects help?
- Within your organization how are project priorities decided. Is the pattern at top and lower levels the same or different. Which should it be?
- What constitutes project success in your part of the organization?
- Are people rewarded for successful projects?
- To what extent are project problems and issues either technical or ones of management?

- To what extent have past project objectives and performance indicators both been identified at the project planning stage, and found later to have been correct and appropriate - rather than changed later?

- Are the right research projects done? Is the amount of research right?

7 FEASIBILITY

7.1 Introduction to Feasibility

Investigating whether or not something is practicable and possible is itself an action. The action may be so big as to be treated as a project or phase, or so small as to be a brief discussion. This chapter later describes the action as though a phase, so its 'tasks' can be discussed, but frequently in common sense practice for a small action most of these 'tasks' would be done mentally.

A **Feasibility Study** (**FS**) is one or the other of:

- a part of the detailed planning step within a management cycle of some previously agreed larger action, which we call **implicit FS**

- an action in its own right; with its own management cycle of planning it, doing it, and reviewing and controlling it; perhaps with its own terms of reference (TOR), meeting and working papers; which we call **explicit FS**.

An implicit FS can arise in the planning step of the management cycle of any level of action, e.g. of a development, a phase, a task or an activity. So it can arise at any such level within any of Analysis, User Design, Technical Design, Implementation and Maintenance.

In many such cases the implicit FS becomes just an informal discussion. 'Well, that way would take several days, which we can't afford, but this way should only take a few hours.' The only permanent record may be just a message left, say, in a data dictionary or in a comment in a program or data.

Explicit FS involves the undertaking of a formal investigation with working papers and formal approval procedures. For such an investigation, the terms of reference should be specified and a report on the exercise and its outcome should be produced.

A FS as presented here is *not* prescribed as a prerequisite to any particular planning, management or development phase. Rather, *it may be undertaken at any point.* Three situations for a FS are suggested later, in Section 7.6.

The nature and extent of the study will also vary in accordance with the particular application area and circumstances. Only *general* guidelines and recommendations are given.

In the following text, three classes of personnel are identified - users, managers and the FS team. In some cases, such a distinction may exist while in others, the FS team may itself comprise members of the other two classes. The chapter should therefore be read accordingly.

Feasibility investigation usually goes on continually, taken up whenever appropriate. It should be intellectually honest. Problems may arise when the decision makers do not have the time, personality or ability to do required feasibility studies themselves. Opportunities for bias, e.g. from conscious or subconscious political motives, arise in evaluating and reporting a feasibility study.

People loosely say 'feasible' for different kinds of practicable or possible:

- what is theoretically possible (= *theoretically feasible*)
- what is possible using existing technology (= *technically feasible*)
- what is possible using existing installed equipment, e.g. with a currently available software package (= feasible with current system)
- what is *worthwhile*, i.e. justifiable from benefits against costs (= *economically feasible*)
- what is managerially or politically acceptable; what one could get away with (= managerially feasible?)
- what is easy to achieve (misleading use of the term)
- what is likely to happen (misleading)
- what is likely to be 'successful' - though 'success' maybe difficult to define (misleading)
- what people will accept, e.g. what users would accept (misleading).

7.2 Framework Diagram

The main feasibility tasks may be sequenced as shown in Figure 7.1.

The lines show alternative paths through the tasks. Only those along one path are done. The task of evaluation of assumptions is not needed in most situations, as explained in Section 7.6.

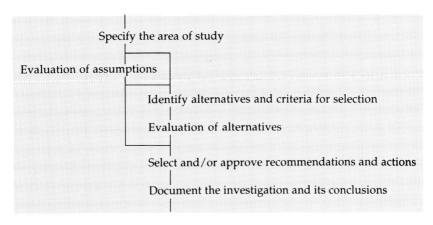

Specify the area of study

Evaluation of assumptions

Identify alternatives and criteria for selection

Evaluation of alternatives

Select and/or approve recommendations and actions

Document the investigation and its conclusions

Figure 7.1

7.3 Definition

A **feasibility study** means the actions to determine whether one or more proposed methods of working seem practicable and justifiable. The *proposals* may include both suggested improvements as changes to current methods of working and introduction of new methods. Generally there may be *several alternatives.* Within each main alternative there will be many detailed variants, but that detail is not relevant in the feasibility study.

A feasibility study usually starts with a general investigation of the problem. This leads to the identification of possible alternatives, each of which is assessed for technical, operational and economic feasibility. Criteria for assessment of the alternatives, selection between them, and decision making must either exist previously or be established.

Generally people study the main alternative solutions to a need or problem that has already been perceived. One alternative is to make no change.

The *justification* usually expects one or more of:
• improved income
• reduced expenditure
• better service, including speed and timing
• better safety
• continuing or improved employment and welfare
• better decision making
• better availability and presentation of relevant information

- better use of resources and assets.

Expected costs and benefits may be once-off and regular. Benefits include improving services and products and reducing expenditure. There may be *once-off* development and installation costs and income from sale of freed assets. There may be *regular* operating and maintenance costs and operating benefits. Most alternatives include development and change-over costs which have to be incurred before the longer-term benefits. The costs and benefits are uncertain, initially unknown.

The relevant *methods of working* may include human, computerized and automatic procedures and processes. These may form one or many information systems, together with planning, decision making and control methods.

The purpose is to reduce the uncertainty that would otherwise exist about some decision. We return to this in Section 7.6.

The development of complex systems may need several feasibility studies. Each study may be explicit or implicit, and formal, informal or a judicious mixture, depending on the mix of the uncertainty and the near-certainty.

Feasibility evaluation is a continual activity of people conscientiously looking out for realistic opportunities for improvements.

Those who suggest, those who assess and those who decide must be intellectually honest. Human integrity, with open, frank and effective communication may sow the seeds of success. Commercial viability must be correctly assessed. The temptation to arrogant opinion, with the fallibilities of careless or deliberate incompleteness and inadequate justification may lead to misjudgement and fruitless work.

7.4 Objectives

The general aim is usually:
- to determine whether or not a proposed information system should be developed
- to determine whether proposed alterations to an existing system should be made
- if there are several alternatives, then to select the best.

The objectives are that within reasonable or previously stated resources, time-scale and terms of reference:
- each alternative is evaluated sufficiently, so that recommendations between them can be made confidently

- decisions between the alternatives are made appropriately and correctly
- the selected solution's justification should be adequately documented and the appropriate major products produced.

7.5 Scope

Each alternative and combination of alternatives should be investigated only sufficiently far to convince the decision makers either how unlikely it is to be cost-effective, viable, and technically and managerially feasible, or how likely it is to be beneficial and to convince them of the various benefits. For each feasibility study the resources - including time-scale, costs and personnel - should be based on the alternatives to be considered and the importance to the organization of the proposed project and likely developments. The resources committed to evaluating each alternative should be based on its likely benefits - e.g. cost-effectiveness and so on as above.

The more likely alternatives should be studied more fully. The politics and human relations aspects of decision making should be borne in mind - not becoming subservient to resources for studying only the technical aspects of each alternative.

7.6 Prerequisites

The only prerequisite is that an explicit FS should have worded the terms of reference well, giving the purpose and objectives of the study.

It is important that the purpose of the study be stated, regardless of whether it is to be an implicit or explicit study.

The purpose is to reduce uncertainty when making some decision or decisions. There are three situations. These have different prerequisites.

1   The FS has been requested so as to produce a list of:
- suggestions which become alternatives

- the assumptions of each alternative

- criteria to be borne in mind

- under which criteria and assumptions each alternative is best.

Here the TOR are open-ended: the assumptions and criteria for selection are not given, and the FS team are free to invent new alternatives, assumptions and criteria within reason. The objective is to determine possible alternatives, e.g. for future directions. This situation includes decision-analysis exercises of the form 'what if ...'.

2   The FS has been requested at a BSP or ISSP decision. This is happening before deciding on a major course of action, e.g. some policy change, some IS change, some new IS or some major rearrangement of ISs. The FS objectives then include ascertaining that the stated assumptions - and any unstated ones that may have been missed - in the formulation of the course of action are valid; essentially guaranteeing that the course of action is practicable with no unforeseen major problems.

3   The FS objective is solely to decide between two or more alternatives before doing further work. The situation arises frequently within the planning of a lower-level phase, task or activity. That phase, task or activity work must be done as part of some already-approved development or project. Choices between various alternative techniques and tools or between alternative actions using different resources must be made. No assumptions need evaluation. The people involved should know their environment and hence the criteria for selection. Such implicit FS is usually small and can be done informally and quickly.

In principle the first two of these three situations can be mixed. Also poorly described alternatives may need clarification and accurate definition.

In situations 1 and 2 the FS team will welcome guidance. They will usually need a variety of other information, such as whichever is appropriate from the following:

• information needed for calculating costs and benefits. For example if doing calculations of not present values or discounted rates of return: what rates of inflation (escalation) and interest should be assumed; and what should be allowed for overheads (situation 2)

• information about current BSP, ISSP and the organization generally

• information about external developments in fields such as information systems, information technology, techniques and tools

• privacy policy, e.g. whether the FS is confidential

• assumptions about future users and developers, e.g. skills, locations, environment, requirements in outline

• who requested the FS and why; how its recommendations are likely to be interpreted and used.

For situation 3 the people involved should know their project and where to find prerequisite information.

If appropriate, suitable guidelines should be provided which would better enable the investigators to do their task.

7.7 Tasks

Only certain tasks below apply to each situation.

1   Specify the area of study.

2   Evaluate the assumptions.

3   Identify alternatives and criteria for selection.

4   Evaluate the alternatives.

Tasks 2, 3 and 4 are not mutually exclusive. One may lead to another. The purpose of distinguishing them is to facilitate the purpose and scope of the study. If decisions have been made there may be little purpose in identifying alternative courses of action.

5   Select recommendations.

6   Document the investigation and its conclusions.

7.8 Major Product

The main product should be:

• Feasibility study report.

There may be a progress report, e.g. if the FS is a recognized project.

7.9 Task Descriptions

You should read these descriptions as appropriate to each situation.

7.9.1 Specify the Area of Study

The aim of this task is to define the current position and the perceived problems. These should all be described in some common form so that consistent evaluations and decisions about feasibility can be made.

Where, as in situation 2, the FS arises within ISSP or ISTP to assess the feasibility of a particular suggested information system development, or a major change to an existing system, the following comments and activities may be appropriate.

Obtain the current terms of reference (TOR). Establish the FS team's reporting structures within the TOR and the Strategic Planning Report.

Set up an interview schedule and a detailed work plan for the feasibility study. The FS team should be thoroughly familiar with the organization and its current policies. Otherwise in parallel with these activities the FS team need to study background materials and understand the main problems affecting the organization.

The analysis of main functional areas is a development of the analysis of major functional areas defined in the strategic planning phase. The feasibility study will normally encompass a specific business area of the organization, though this area may be a very wide one and may expand in scope over time. The FS team should have or develop hierarchical function charts and input and output diagrams, but at a less detailed level than will be created later at the analysis stage. The aim is to increase the FS team's and future system developers' understanding of requirements.

The FS team need:

- a description of the key activities to be supported by the potential system

- a statement of the modes of interaction expected, e.g. batch cycles, online response, clerical interfaces, data distribution, ownership and other measurable criteria.

The analysis of information required by the main functional areas implies creating some documentation about the types and volumes of information to be handled within the main activities. The aim is a broad brush picture of the information types, flows and processes envisaged.

An assessment of the current system, whether that system is already a computer system or not, is a vital activity. This assessment should include the cost and quality of service of the current system. It is necessary to identify where any problems with the existing system lie, not least because one alternative may be that of 'no change'. This needs a statement of the problems and issues perceived by management, e.g. that the service is not good enough in particular ways, e.g. which parts cost too much, what is too slow, what is unreliable, and which particular information is not available. The list of problems will also be relevant in choosing the criteria for selecting solutions for the future.

The aim of these four areas of work is to lead to a summary statement of requirements which can be checked with the future users and management. It is also necessary to comment on the level of uncertainty or fuzziness that may still be apparent in the requirements. As well as this, the potential phasing of developments for sub-groups of the requirements for stepwise implementation should be considered. The FS team may need a work plan involving a sequence of interviews with managers and other staff of the various functional areas before they can evaluate the feasibility of various alternatives and their development phasing.

7.9.2 Evaluation of Assumptions

This task is undertaken in situation 2 in response to some decision to investigate a particular course of action. This could be an IS development; or to distribute certain processing; to purchase a data dictionary; or to use a particular methodology.

Such decisions are generally taken in response to some conditions, problems, and/or recommendations from managers, hardware and software vendors or consultants. Such decisions are generally supported with some notional allocation of resources.

The objective of a FS in such a case would be to establish the premise on which the decisions are based and accordingly assess the resources allocated.

Such an exercise requires interviewing the decision makers in the first instance. This inquiry should establish the assumptions on which the decisions are based.

The next activity should be to determine the appropriate resources, if those allocated are inappropriate. Expert help should sought, if necessary.

The FS should investigate the assumptions underlying the course of action, e.g. would IS developers really benefit from and use the new facilities. The major assumptions, for example given in the situation or TOR, should have already been thought out, but some minor assumptions may have been missed or unstated.

7.9.3 Identify Alternatives and Criteria for Selection

The identification of alternatives tends to be a very subjective matter. Often the list to be considered is too narrow in scope, and fundamental technical alternatives are ignored. The following check list suggests some directions in which alternatives could be sought:

- 'no change' option: continue present system
- patching the present system
- prototype the new system: 'quick and dirty'
- batch only
- basically batch with only data entry and queries online
- distributed or centralized

- use of an application package.

Alternative software such as teleprocessing monitors, data dictionary systems (DDS), database management system (DBMS), and query and report languages could also be considered as options at this stage. A DBMS decision could be deferred until after the full detailed analysis work is done, when the nature of the data structure and requirements are better understood. However, a good policy over the use of a data dictionary in the analysis stage may prove valuable, since a data dictionary system suitable for analysis and design and capable of being integrated with a DBMS may be preferred.

The list of criteria for choosing between alternatives should be agreed with the user management. Some common **criteria** are:

- degree of matching user needs and expectations; users being of four main types:
  - input
  - decision maker
  - report reader
  - maintainer
- cost/benefit saving for the organization
- development costs
- development time-scales
- operational costs for the data-processing service
- confidence level in technical feasibility
- confidence level in development time-scale
- interfaces between ISs, including existing systems
- organization upset level.

7.9.4 Evaluation of Alternatives

This should be a formal exercise, preferably leading to an analysis table showing the performance of the alternatives against each criterion. A weighting system such as is commonly used in hardware or software selection studies could be used. DAP is an example (Section 4.9 item 6).

The measures used are of four main types:

- *technical*, i.e. is the alternative technologically possible
- *organizational*, i.e. what is the probable impact on the organization's structures
- *effort and time-scale*, i.e. can the solution be implemented within the time-scales given and within the human resources available
- *cost/benefit*. There are two aspects in the cost/benefit assessment of a particular alternative. The first is to evaluate the total cost of a particular alternative by combining all individual costs using

statistical techniques. The other aspect is to establish where the proposed alternative stands within the continuous spectrum which range from a maximum-cost 'ideal' service solution to a low-cost poor service solution.

We strongly recommend that an assessment of risk should be included; one method of doing this is to use '3-point' estimates, i.e.:

- what if all goes well?
- what if we assume the normal clogging factors?
- what if there is a series of disasters?

There are standard methods to combine such estimates, e.g. within PERT and risk analysis. Simulation and decision trees may help.

The FS team should call upon expert help, where appropriate, in the assessment of the alternative solutions considered.

7.9.5 Select Recommendations

The outcome of the study should enable appropriate decisions to be taken. These may take the form of either formal recommendations to the initiators of the study or the pursuance of a particular course of action, where the study is conducted by the decision makers.

7.9.6 Document the Investigation and its Conclusions

It is desirable to document the FS and its findings, regardless of whether it is an implicit or explicit study. The report may guide future investigations as well as providing a record as to why particular decisions were taken.

This task culminates in the Feasibility Report itself which is presented to the managers or steering committee. The contents should reflect the previous stages of the work, and there should be a section - repeated in the introduction or management summary - which makes it clear what the managers or steering committee are being recommended to do and by when. For example the alternative of no action, i.e. continuing the current practice, may be losing the organization £100 000 per month relative to the safe alternative being recommended, but for which a grant can only be obtained if the organization applies for it by a certain date.

A feasibility study should recommend one alternative or a short list of alternative solutions from which the management can make the final selection. If, however, user nominees have been working actively on the feasibility study and have been able to bring an accurate representation of the user management objectives, then the feasibility study could recommend one single solution.

The following three tasks may or may not occur.

7.9.7 Select or Approve Solution

This is an activity for the management rather than for the feasibility study team itself and is not considered further here.

7.9.8 Update Terms of Reference

A change in the terms of reference might become necessary in the light of information gathered during the feasibility study. If this is the case, then the terms of reference must be updated and a new TOR produced.

7.9.9 Document the Chosen Solution and Work Plan

Once the decision has been made, the study team should prepare a final report on the chosen solution, the main objective being to publish more details of the work plan that were available in the main Feasibility Report. This then provides a starting point for subsequent analysis stage.

7.10 Major Product Description

Feasibility Study Report

The document should cover the following:

- statement of the *purpose* of the study: this may also include the names of the initiators of the study and the study team, together with a statement of the reasons that led to the study
- statement of the *procedures* followed in the study
- statement of the *areas examined* by the study
- statement of the *findings* of the study
- statement of any *recommendations* - the rationale for these recommendations should be outlined
- any additional *comments*, including any lessons learnt and pointers to future studies.

7.11 Resources

Two kinds of people are needed to carry out a feasibility study:

- a nominated team of people who can cross the bridge between technical computer-oriented staff and end-users. One from each side could be considered if at least one person has *good* knowledge of the other side. The size of the team should, however, be related to other factors such as the time-scale and size of the project
- consulted experts providing advice to the team on user department practice, financial evaluation, programming, database, teleprocessing and clerical procedures.

The team should ideally be composed of people who are independent of the decision makers and the impact of the outcome of the study, i.e. objective investigators and observers. They should be assisted by those who have to make the decisions, representatives of those who will implement the decisions and representatives of those affected by the decisions. Additionally, expert advice should be sought where necessary.

The objective should be to achieve a complete yet balanced coverage.

7.12 Techniques and tools

Methods for PERT and resource allocation; calculations of net present value and discounted rate of return; and a methodology for establishing requirements, e.g. BSP, BIAIT, may be needed.

7.13 General Comments

Formal feasibility studies will have working papers and formal approval procedures. Informal studies will simply be a record of what was done, what the decision was and the rationales.

7.14 References and Sources

MADD73: Maddison, R. N. Feasibility of Computer Projects. PM951: *Computing and Computers: Computability*. The Open University Press (1973) pp49-60. Now (1988) out of print and will never be reprinted.

7.15 Project Control

General project control procedures should be applied to the feasibility studies especially in the case where they are lengthy and formal and when the feasibility team is large.

In both formal and informal studies there is a need to monitor continually the feasibility of system development against changes in the business and environment.

IV DEVELOPMENT PHASES

8 ANALYSIS

8.1 Introduction to Analysis

Tactical planning of a new information system development project is usually followed by analysis, here ignoring project planning which every project has. But some overview analysis may also be required within ISSP.

An analysis phase involves gathering information from several sources, e.g. interviews, questionnaires and studying existing documents. The aim is to understand and to document better particular aspects of requirements and existing systems, the particular aspects may be for a particular area.

The temptation to slip into design too early should be resisted, to avoid pre-empting views that may arise later in the analysis. Completeness and consistency are essential to avoid wasteful development actions based on misleading scant muddles.

Different methodologies use different terms, techniques, tools and tasks, as illustrated in [MADD83ISM]. We found it impossible to write this chapter in a form that was unbiased and free from detailed terms of any particular methodology. So you must mentally replace our terms, definitions, objectives, tasks and products by those of your methodology where appropriate.

8.2 Framework Diagram

In Figure 8.1 no sequencing between the four types of analysis is implied. They can be done concurrently and incrementally and in parallel.

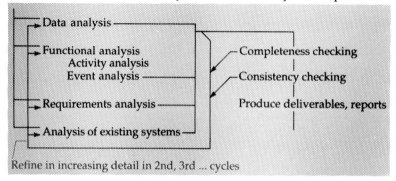

Figure 8.1

We have shown the following types of analysis, to be done in any sequence and with incremental refinement giving evolution of the analysis deliverables.

Data analysis is the discovery of the main types of information and data of the organization undergoing analysis.

Functional analysis is the identification of the basic functions which the business is required to perform to meet its business objectives; it consists of two parts:

- **Activity analysis,** i.e. the analysis of the business operations
- **Event analysis,** i.e. the analysis of events which determine the business operations performed.

Requirements analysis is the discovery of the requirements any users have.

Analysis of *existing* systems.

These types of analysis are continued as required until the deliverables become consistent and complete.

8.3 Definition

Analysis is the decomposition and comprehension of the relevant parts of an organization. It can be applied to:

- the existing business systems
- the required business systems and to each of:
- the types of information used by the business
- the types of functions, activities and events of the business
- the types of information flows
- the types of possible processes and events that can occur during the life of an entity with which the organization deals.

Analysis is concerned with *what is required*, and not the method of implementing solutions. The purpose of the analysis phase is to gain a thorough understanding of the business and its requirements, and to record information about both of these. This information must be recorded in a manner which assists design decisions and promotes a flexible, maintainable design. Generally this may mean any combination from the following kinds of analysis. Different methodologies recommend different combinations of these kinds of analysis, of the detailed lists within them, and with differing emphasis. It would be difficult to write this chapter in wording that fits every methodology, so we have not attempted that. You should interpret our words here to mean *the equivalents in the methodology in use* in the IS development in the organization. You should realize we drop the word 'type' where the meaning should be clear.

Analyse the relevant end-users' requirements in increasing detail to document each type of:

- event
- activity, including manual and computerized operations and processes
- information that exists or is held, e.g. information base, data store
- information flow
- access to information; e.g. retrieval, creation, change and deletion, with entry points and access paths
- organizational responsibility, including functional area structure and reporting structure
- time interval, e.g. when or how frequently...
- interrelationships between the above.

Analyse the relevant parts of the existing system similarly, if not already analysed.

Analyse all main types of information and data in all areas, including other areas that may be relevant for flexibility and ease of future changes. This data analysis is essentially independent of current use and information flows. The types of information may include business entities, properties, facts, associations, relationships, attributes, roles, identifiers and functional dependencies.

Prepare a detailed specification of all types of activity, information, information and data flow, and access that are to be provided by the proposed system. This functional specification may include any combination of the following:

- which events trigger which activities, processes, operations and information flows
- which activity completions are associated with which events
- the inputs to each activity, process and operation
- the outputs from each process, the corresponding information needed to be either input or stored, and algorithms - functional information interface diagrams or equivalents, e.g. as lists, that show detailed information flows between each activity within each functional area
- a total information interface diagram or equivalent showing information flows between functional areas
- constraints for consistency and integrity, including sequencing and existence rules
- privacy requirements
- the associations between functional areas and activities.

Specify the performance, response time, availability, reliability, security, responsibility and control features required. These can be specified either here as part of analysis or as part of user design.

Cross-match all the above, e.g. check that all information needed for each activity is available, that all data can be created and deleted, and that all activities can be triggered.

Many methodologies and representations for the above have been proposed and used successfully.

8.4 Objectives

By the end of the analysis phase the following should have been achieved for the relevant area of the organization.

1   The functional and information requirements of the proposed information systems to support the users' needs have been defined and documented.

2   These requirements have been refined if necessary to a level sufficient to enable work to proceed on any subsequent decisions and design phases, and described in appropriate deliverables.

3   All other products giving information required for any subsequent decision points and design phases have been produced.

8.5 Scope

1   The area of the business to be investigated is defined by the appropriate plans.

2   This phase defines the functional and information requirements of the area under investigation.

3   It also analyses the systems currently employed within the area under investigation.

4   The analysis of data should cover an area which is broader than that required for any information systems proposed in the feasibility study, to ensure flexibility for the future. The area and depth of analysis is delimited, primarily, by the limit of interaction of the data to be used in the information system and the operations upon it; also constraints may be placed on the area by the plans.

5   The analysis should, as far as possible, be free from considerations concerning implementation details and especially those affecting computerization. Decisions should not be made on how functions will be implemented or where data will be recorded. There should be no assumptions such as that any part of the system will, necessarily, be computerized or be manual. Such decisions belong in the design phases. Later iterations of analysis, after some design has occurred, can take into account some of the consequential results; however, care must be taken in the manner in which these affect the analysis results.

8.6 Prerequisites

1   Resources committed to the project, both user and data-processing personnel.
2   Project Steering Committee established.
3   Signed Terms of Reference.
4   Development time-scales for this and subsequent phases.
5   Feasibility study report.

8.7 Task List

1   Data Analysis
2   Functional Analysis
2.1   Activity Analysis
2.2   Event Analysis
3   Requirements Analysis
4   Analysis of Existing Systems
5   Completeness Checking
6   Consistency Checking
7   Production of Reports
7.1   Production of Functional Specifications
7.2   Production of Management Report.

8.8 Major Products List

1   Progress and Exception Report
2   Functional Specifications
3   Function Charts
4   Conceptual Data Models
5   Information Flow Diagrams
6   Other data-function mapping models
7   Business Function Model
8   Requirements Report.

8.9 Task Descriptions

Analysis can be carried out in various ways, but the approach adopted should encompass all the tasks described below. The sequence of performing the tasks should be similar to that shown in the framework diagram in Section 8.2, but this is by no means essential, nor need the work be subdivided in the manner given below. The analysis process is usually one of continual iteration, refinement and backtracking until a set of results is achieved that is satisfactory to the users and analysts.

1 Data Analysis

Analyse all the main types of information and data concerned with the area under investigation, and any other areas that may be relevant for future flexibility. The boundary of investigation is drawn primarily by the limit of interaction of the data found and its usage. Data analysis is essentially independent of current use, information flows and company organization. The types of information recorded may include:

- business entities and their properties, attributes and roles
- business facts
- data identifiers
- functional dependencies of the data
- intrinsic relationships between business entities.

2 Functional Analysis

Identify the basic functions which the business is required to perform to meet the business objectives of the area under investigation. Functional analysis consists of two parts, e.g. *in some methodologies:*

2.1 Activity Analysis

Discover the business operations and functions which determine the way in which the organization operates in the areas concerned.

2.2 Event Analysis

Discover the events which determine the way in which the business operations and functions are undertaken. Two types of events must be found:

- real-time, i.e. time-dependent events
- 'random' events due to internal and external influences.

Random events can be either internal or external. Activity and event analysis should produce results which are interrelated, e.g. the events which trigger a function; these must be correlated for the functions identified to produce the results for functional analysis.

The types of information recorded may include:

- function name and purpose
- the events which trigger the function
- the events triggered by the function
- the information created, altered and used by the function
- who should be responsible for the function
- skills required to perform the function
- where the function should be performed
- whether and how events can cause interruptions of actions.

3 Requirements Analysis

Investigate problems with current systems and find out in detail what users want from any new systems. Collect more detailed information about the requirements, e.g. by interviewing user representatives and by questionnaires. The information collected may include:

- business algorithms, e.g. method of calculating derived data items
- timing requirements of functions
- dependence of function on other functions
- expected frequency of carrying out, i.e. execution, of each function and frequency of events occurring
- data privacy requirements
- data integrity requirements
- number of occurrences of information types, e.g. expected number of entities, of relationship occurrences, and so on.

4 Analysis of Existing Systems

Analyse the systems, both computerized and manual, currently employed within the area under investigation, in order to:

- gain a thorough understanding of the current business practices
- find out which processes are already automated
- find out which processes are currently performed and where any problems are, e.g. organizational difficulties, system bottlenecks
- determine which data is already held in a machine-readable form.

5 Completeness Checking

Perform tests to discover if the results produced from preceding analysis tasks, i.e. 1 to 4, are complete. This is discovered by correlating the various results to see if all the information required is present. For example some information might be missing from one task as it is dependent on another task. Every analysis task continually produces new results and refines existing results. The information necessary to refine existing results will possibly come from a different task and will, probably, be a new result of the task that produced it. In completeness checking, the various information needed is discovered and either the new information will already have been found, or a new cycle of analysis is started to find it.

6 Consistency Checking

Perform tests to discover if the complete results produced are consistent. If not a new cycle of analysis will be started to make them so. The sort of checking carried out is to test that all information needed for a function is available; that all data items can be created, modified or deleted; that all functions are triggered by an event, and so on. Consistency will be verified by analysing the mappings between all the information produced in preceding tasks. Consistency and completeness checking are very similar in character and may be done at the same time. The types of information which may be recorded include:

- the interaction between a function and the data model, e.g. entry points and access paths showing the usage of properties and attributes by functions
- the interaction between a specific data type and the functions it is used in, e.g. Entity Life Cycle and State
- the interaction between events and functions.

7 Production of Reports

Various reports can be produced as a result of analysis. Two of the most important are functional specifications and the management report.

7.1 Production of the Functional Specification

Prepare the detailed specification of the proposed system as described in Section 8.10.2. Many parts of the specification will have already been prepared whilst performing the earlier tasks. Some parts of the specification may already be held on the data dictionary.

7.2 Production of the Management Report

Prepare the Progress and Exception Report for management. This should also include a résumé of the information needed for any subsequent decisions. As in Task 7.1, many parts of the report will have already been prepared.

8.10 Major Product Descriptions

1 Progress and Exception Report

This report is maintained through the life of the system. It will eventually include documentation of subsequent decisions and of amendments to statements and decisions made earlier in the life of the system, in the light of work done in this phase.

2 Functional Specifications

There is one specification for each business function identified and one specification as summary. The specification may be a combination of free text, structured text and/or diagrams. The functions which are specified may be operational or management functions. The documentation includes the events which trigger the function, the purpose of the function and the types of information, e.g. attributes, relationships and entities, that are acted on by the function.

3 Function Charts

These charts are often drawn in the form of a matrix or several such to show the connections between:

- functions and departments
- skills
- location
- events.

Another commonly used form of function chart is a function hierarchy; this depicts all known functions arranged in a hierarchy of functions and their sub-functions.

4 Conceptual Data Model

This documents the data objects, i.e. the entities of the business and their inherent structure. Examples of types of conceptual data models are the Relational model and the Entity-Attribute-Relationship model. A model may be constructed depicting the connections between data objects and locations. This can be as a table or a matrix, giving information to aid in decisions concerning distribution, e.g. should the system be distributed and, if so, what should be distributed where?

5 Information Flow Diagrams

These show the information created and used by each function and the source and destination of information which passes outside the boundaries of the area under investigation. The reasons for the flows may be specified. Diagrams for new functions may be drawn at the conceptual level. Diagrams for existing information systems may be drawn at both the implemented logical level and the conceptual level, if these will be useful. Some people call them **Data Flow Diagrams**.

6 Other Data-to-Function mapping models

There are various other diagrams which depict the mappings between data and the business functions which use that data, e.g. Function/Data matrices, Entity Life Cycle diagrams and Access Path diagrams. These show the data which is used by a function or the way in which data is affected by various functions; i.e. they show the interactions between data and functions and vice-versa. Other possibilities for diagrams include:

- input-output diagrams
- flow-process diagrams
- activity-sequence diagrams
- control-loop diagrams - as in Section 11.2 of this book
- influence and multi-cause diagrams - showing what causes what.

7 Business Function Model

This depicts the mapping of business functions to organizational business objectives. The form of the model may be similar to that in the BSP and ISSP, but at a more detailed level. This may be a matrix structure or lists.

8 User Requirements Specification

This should be a statement in detail of the users' requirements in their language and terms, and with explanation of those terms for the implementors.

8.11 Resources

Although there will be some costs and computing facilities, the main resources required are the right people and suitable software.

1 People

End-users, including end-user management, who are responsible for, and perform, the functions under investigation. Systems Analysts and business analysts rather than application designers.

2 Software

A data dictionary system is practically essential for large projects, and very useful for smaller ones. Prototyping software often would be useful. Automated diagramming software is a great facilitator.

8.12 Techniques and Tools

We describe the techniques and tools (t & t) for each task separately.

1 Data Analysis t & t

Entity modelling and normalization may be very useful for modelling and manipulating the results discovered by the interviews with users and inspection of existing documentation.

2 Functional Analysis t & t

Data flow analysis and functional decomposition can model and manipulate the results of this analysis and also guide in the discovery of further results. Other methods of recording the results include Structured English, and Problem Statement Language/Problem Statement Analyzer, PSL/PSA.

3 Requirements Analysis t & t

The techniques used for this analysis will be similar to those used in (1) and (2) above, the results of which can be used to guide further analysis. Frequency and volume information can be discovered by interview and inspection of existing documentation and systems. Prototyping will be of greatest use in this task.

4 Analysis of Existing Systems t & t

Any existing systems can be analysed by utilizing tasks 8.7.1 to 8.7.6. Therefore the relevant techniques will be the same.

5 Completeness Checking t & t

The techniques used for checking completeness will involve checking the interactions between the results of the various tasks of this phase. For instance, relevant techniques include Access Path Analysis and Entity State Analysis. Data Flow Analysis can be of use here as well.

6 Consistency Checking † & †

The techniques of use here are similar to those employed by completeness checking.

7 Production of Reports t & t

Report-writing techniques and tools or a data dictionary or a simple microcomputer package or word-processing package may help.

The tools which can be used throughout this phase are data dictionaries, prototyping software and automated modelling software, e.g. automated production of diagrams. There are various methodologies in existence which cover some or all of the tasks outlined, e.g. the CRIS1 methodologies [OLLE82]. Tools and techniques which have facilities for integrating together the analysis, design and implementation phases may help improve productivity, though their use maybe cost-effective only in larger information system developments.

Throughout the phase techniques of presenting, of interviewing and of devising and using questionnaires will usually be required.

8.13 General Comments

None.

8.14 References and Sources

• BENY87: D. Benyon & S. Skidmore. Towards a Tool Kit for the Systems Analyst. *Computer J.* Vol 30 No 1 (Feb 1987) pp 1-7.

HOWE84: D.R. Howe. *Data Analysis for Data Base* (sic) *Design*. Edward Arnold (1984).

KLEI87: H.K. Klein & R.A. Hirschheim. A Comparative Framework of Data Modelling Paradigms and Approaches. *Computer J.* Vol 30 No 1 (Feb 1987) pp8-15.

[MADD83ISM], [DDSWP82], [OLLE82] as in Appendix 3.

MART85: J. Martin & C. McClure. *Diagramming Techniques for Analysts and Programmers*. Prentice-Hall (1985).

WOOD82: A.T. Wood-Harper & G. Fitzgerald. A Taxonomy of Current Approaches to Systems Analysis. *Computer J.* Vol 25 No 1 (1982) pp12-16.

WOOD85: A.T. Wood-Harper *et al. Information Systems Definition: The Multiview Approach.* Blackwell (1985).

8.15 Project Control

There are various aims which should be taken into account when planning the control of the Analysis Phase, these being:

1. The major products listed above should be made available, or a report made available which explains why the product cannot be produced.

2. The cost of developing and operating the proposed information system may be calculated, if this is a management requirement at this stage.

3. If there is a decision point between this phase and the next, then any recommendations and supporting documentation should be produced.

4. The resources and time estimated for this phase should not be significantly exceeded. If a data dictionary is in use, rigorous updating standards should be imposed; one of these should be a requirement to place results in the dictionary as soon as possible after they are captured. For a large analysis project the team may be subdivided into groups for each of tasks 1 to 4. Certain members of all the individual groups for tasks 1 to 4 should be chosen to take part in tasks 5 and 6, to ensure a balanced viewpoint in these tasks. Project meetings for project personnel should be scheduled at frequent, regular intervals to correlate results, report on progress and allocate time-scales and assignments. The major products listed above should be made available, in whatever state they are in, for these meetings. User project meetings should also be scheduled at regular intervals to report on progress, answer queries from the users' representatives and receive replies in return; this can be with the Project Steering Committee, or separate and in addition to meetings with it. Interviews with users should usually be arranged by the project management. Access to necessary documents should also be arranged by project management, where possible.

9 USER DESIGN

9.1 Introduction to User Design

To design is a generalized and valuable concept. It covers all aspects of forming diagrams or documents that fully describe what is to be implemented. These aspects include processes and products. The design processes involve significant tasks and activities. The design products are far more detailed than a typical specification of requirements.

User design (**UD**) is oriented towards the end-users. Constraints such as rules of particular hardware and software play no part. There is no question of 'it must be like that to fit the available software'.

But user design is not just about the user procedures that are to be computerized. It includes non-computerized procedures and detailed decisions on the interfaces between them and the computer system. Here is a logical boundary, with information flows across it to be designed. User design also includes security facilities, for example to prevent unauthorized information flows across many logical boundaries, some of which are partly inside and partly outside the computer system boundary.

As soon as a primitive UD product is available it could be turned into a primitive implementation, e.g. a prototype. If technical design (TD) and implementation can be essentially automated then this can be repeated for each user design incremental improvement. This is the value of application information system generators, freeing the designers from repetitive TD and implementation or getting the design right first time.

9.2 Framework Diagram

See Figure 9.1.

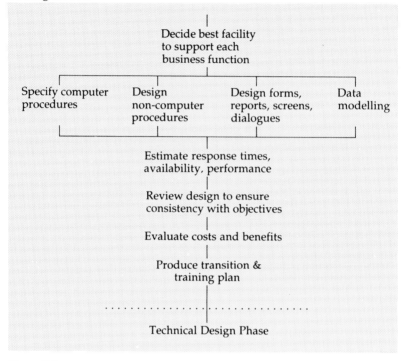

Figure 9.1

9.3 Definition

At this stage of systems development user requirements have been established in terms of functions to be supported and performance required and the system has been modelled conceptually, for example by an information flow diagram, an entity-attribute-relationship model, process models and other products as in Chapter 8. Overall constraints on design are likely to have been clearly established, for example the kinds of hardware and software to be used will have been specified in general terms in the planning phases.

The design activity required in this phase is to match functions to be supported with appropriate facilities that give the performance required within the limits of relevant economic, technical and organizational factors. Non-computer components of the required system will be completely designed in this phase - for example supporting clerical procedures. The computer-based components of the required system will be outlined but not designed; however the interfaces between computer and non-computer procedures must be designed. At the end of this phase the system will have been designed to a sufficient level of detail for the user to perceive clearly its operational features and thus have an opportunity to approve the design.

Some degree of further data modelling may be performed in this phase. For example, if the analysis phase produced a conceptual data model that shows entities and relationships and most but not all attributes, then these should be added in this user design phase.

If the analysis data model is 'global', i.e. covers more systems than the one currently being designed, then this is an appropriate point at which to produce a local view. This is a new task, but it does not create further entities.

In other areas of engineering it is common practice to build a *prototype* for assessment at this user design stage. This has the great advantage of allowing simulated use of the system and makes it easier to establish whether requirements have been met. Also it is possible that users do not fully understand their requirements until they experience using a system. Use of a prototype encourages quite valid iterations of the analysis and user design cycle. Prototyping has not hitherto been widely used in the development of information systems because of the unacceptable cost of implementing a design that might be heavily amended or even rejected. For systems that are to be mass produced, prototyping costs are a small fraction of total development costs and may save the unacceptably high cost of field enhancements or modifications. Information systems are typically one-off and prototype development has not been thought an acceptable addition to total development costs. Nevertheless the high maintenance costs of many systems is a result of going live with what was no more than a prototype. For a prototype approach to be managerially acceptable, the trial prototype should cost far less than the final deliverable, thus it may not be subject to all the quality standards of a conventional system since parts of it will be discarded.

The availability of software tools specifically intended for low-cost system implementation has altered the situation. Prototyping may be particularly valuable in user design where establishing the users' requirements has been found difficult. For example an innovatory system may have no existing well-defined statement of requirements; another possibility is that the users' information needs may be unpredictable or evolving, such as in managerial or decision support applications.

Prototyping may not be worthwhile in a routine well-understood application area.

The extent to which end-users and their managers can or should participate in the design of information systems is an important issue. One extreme possibility is that users do not participate at all, and are presented with a system designed by experts in information technology who may have little experience in the application area. This design approach has happened too often in the past but nowadays is unlikely to be publicly advocated. It is discouraged because it may lead to end-user resentment, resistance to the use of the system, development of unofficial alternative systems, sabotage of the system and eventual early obsolescence of the system.

At the other extreme is the movement toward user managers planning their own systems development and taking responsibility for successful project completion, and lower-level users or even managers taking an active role in designing aspects of their own systems. Recent technological developments that make this form of user participation feasible include the availability of application and system generators and low-cost microprocessor-based systems. Greater degrees of user participation may well improve the users' commitment to the system after implementation, and increase their understanding of costs of enhancements. This form of design should not mean 'carte blanche' for the uncontrolled development of stand-alone systems.

9.4 Objectives

The objectives are to:

- design a system that meets user requirements within planning and policy constraints
- present the design in such a way that the end-users or their representatives can clearly see how the system will operate and agree to subsequent implementation
- provide adequate specification of the system to enable more detailed technical design to take place
- plan for transition and training requirements.

9.5 Scope

From a fully detailed specification of user requirements a design is produced that defines inputs, outputs and processes in a way that makes it clear how the system will appear to the user in terms of facilities and performance. No decisions on technical design are taken but sufficient detail is specified to enable this to happen in the next phase.

Ergonomics, health, safety, welfare and environmental issues may need attention.

9.6 Prerequisites

Before user design for a particular area can start, one needs:

1 Specification of user requirements in terms of functions to be supported, data flow, information base or data storage, entry points and access paths to stored data, processing requirements, performance requirements.

2 Policy covering hardware, software, applications architecture, data storage and retrieval, development. Policy guidelines on the resources available.

Generally the details of requirements come from analysis products. The policies come from ISSP, ISTP and ISPP.

9.7 Tasks

1 Decide the best facility to support each function. This implies the users' view of an overall system architecture. This may include detailed decisions on exactly what is to be computerized and what is not, and also on how the information system will look to the various users. But the general overall policy of what is to be computerized was produced in the ISSP and ISTP.

2 Design the computer procedures. This means produce detailed logical specifications of programs, interfaces, dialogues, menus, processing rules and procedures.

3 Design the non-computer procedures, including auditing controls and user controls. Alternatively, these three tasks could be done by coding, implementing and testing a prototype.

4 Design and specify in detail the input forms, reports and screen layouts.

5 Finish the global data model for the information system.

6   Estimate response times, availability and performance criteria required.

7   Review the design to ensure consistency with objectives.

8   Evaluate the costs and benefits of the system as now defined.

9   Produce a transition and training plan.

10   Produce UD progress and exception report.

9.8 Major Products

1   User design specification.

2   Transition and training plan.

9.9 Task Descriptions

The analysis phase should have defined a conceptual system that meets user requirements. The design of a new system involves matching the requirements of the conceptual system to a set of resources, e.g. people and equipment. Policy guidelines on the resources available for the system will have been established in the ISSP phase. Therefore, the first task in user design is to decide the most suitable facility to support each function. Facility means some human and/or technical resource, for example an interactive terminal or a personal computing facility. Procedures to be performed by computer should be specified but not designed in detail since this is the task of the technical design phase that follows this UD phase. Clerical procedures must be designed in detail however; and also the interfaces between the users and the computers, e.g. forms, screens and reports.

The analysis phase should have provided conceptual data and process models to some degree of detail. In the User Design phase these may have to be elaborated and interpreted to enable database or file design to take place in the technical design phase. For example there may be rules about scheduling and concurrency. The sequences in which users want to supply information to the computer system may be different from the sequence of the corresponding real-world events.

Once the first-cut, i.e. primitive, user design is complete, its likely performance characteristics should be assessed for consistency with the user requirements and a re-evaluation made of costs and benefits. This assessment may be performed by prototyping the design. At the user design phase of an information system development the implications for transition to the new system should be clear and an appropriate transition plan produced. Training will be an important part of transition.

9.10 Major Product Descriptions

1 User Design Specification

The processing method for each function to be supported must be clearly defined together with processing rules, input and output formats and access to stored data. The logical structure of stored data must be defined together with privacy, integrity and security requirements. Data volumes must be specified as well as timing and availability requirements. A prototype may form part of a user design specification.

2 Transition and training plan

The following must be scheduled:

- user training
- completion of material required for training
- completion of reference documentation
- data conversion
- changeover.

9.11 Resources

The team should include:

- system designer
- user or user representative.

They may need:

- application generators to produce a prototype, data dictionary
- computer facilities.

9.12 Techniques and Tools

In general the techniques and tools suggested in Section 8.12 are also the relevant ones for user design.

9.13 General Comments

During user design one has to imagine likely technical designs and implementations corresponding to user design alternatives. A primitive user design, saying that a particular future end-user should have a keyboard and screen, does not imply whether the technical design will be a microcomputer or a terminal linked to a larger computer or network. More detailed user design can only follow after a corresponding primitive technical design has been produced, giving a primitive architecture within the ISSP and ISTP policies.

9.14 References and Sources

References in [MADD83ISM] describe various analysis and design methodologies. These references are in Appendix 3.

9.15 Project Control

None.

9.16 Ideas and Suggestions

- To what extent is the design task seen as having sub-systems?
- Separate technology (hardware and software) from administration (handling and co-ordinating the problems and activities) from organizational structure (people and their roles).
- Can end-user representatives be involved more?
- Can end-user representatives be made responsible for success and given the required authority?
- Does the user area already work the way it should work?
- To what extent will a change to an IS be an improvement to an area that already works well or a change needed because an area does not work well?
- What user reactions are expected?

10 TECHNICAL DESIGN

10.1 Introduction to Technical Design

The Technical Design phase represents the final stage of synthesis of the requirements into a complete and detailed specification of a proposed system. The requirements will be compromised by technical limitations. Thus parts of previous phases may need iteration again. Far from being a purely technical exercise, the tasks may involve the designers in considerable tact and diplomacy to explain their proposed amendments.

Technical design also involves carefully selected balances between short-term objectives, such as fast implementation and good response times, as against long-term objectives, such as design flexibility and durability.

10.2 Framework Diagram

See Figure 10.1.

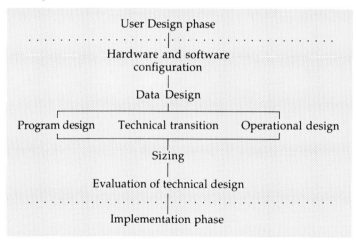

Figure 10.1

In Figure 10.1 the direction down the page does not imply strict task dependencies but indicates the likely starting order of tasks.

10.3 Definition

This phase involves defining precisely how the required system is to be constructed. This is done by designing:

- the hardware and software configuration
- the databases or files
- the programs
- how the proposed system will be operated.

A detailed sizing will also be carried out in this phase.

10.4 Objectives

The objective is to translate the User Design into a satisfactory Technical Design within any constraints imposed elsewhere. This phase involves producing a design which is technically feasible and practical to operate, but is also satisfactorily flexible and durable.

The phase is complete when:

- an operational system has been specified without the need for any more design work
- management approval for the Implementation phase has been obtained.

10.5 Scope

The scope of this phase is the investigations needed for and the making and documenting of all technical decisions about the design of the information system. This covers a variety of types of design: communications equipment; file and database logical design; physical storage structure design; application programs; procedures for security, integrity, dumping, journals, recovery, loading and reloading. It will require methods of proving the correctness of the design and its implementation, and technical documentation of all these, i.e. both the designs and the reasoning.

Some technical design decisions are not relevant to end-users, e.g. which sorting algorithm is to be used. Any choice could meet the users' requirements, and the user does not need to know the choice made. However some decisions, such as to use a particular software package, may affect end-users. For instance, they may need to know details of its commands and facilities, even if such a package will meet their information requirements.

In the light of technical, resource and cost considerations, compromises will have to be made. This may necessitate revisions to the design decisions, possibly made in preceding User and/or Technical Design phase. The compromises and revisions must be properly justified, agreed and documented.

10.6 Prerequisites

1   From the User Design phase:
    - user design specification, including final business data model

    - final business data model

    - transition and training plan.

2   From the Planning phases:
    - hardware and software decisions

    - application architecture report

    - application development plan

    - data storage and retrieval policy

    - development environment policy.

3   From the Analysis phase:
    - function charts.

4   Miscellaneous:
    - appropriate training

    - technical manuals.

10.7 Task List

1   Hardware and software configuration
2   Data design
3   Program design
4   Technical transition design
5   Operational design
6   Sizing
7   Evaluation of technical design

8   Produce TD progress and exception report.

10.8 Major Products List

1   Technical design specification
   • detail system design

   • flow diagram of system and application architecture

   • database and file design

   • program specifications.

2   Revised development plan.

3   Revisions to prerequisites.

4   Operating procedures and instructions.

10.9 Task Descriptions

1 Hardware and Software Configuration

This task involves firming-up on the proposals made in the preceding phases, especially taking note of any User Design decisions. The network design and central hardware products and any in-house systems software to be used is decided. The integration of all Information Technology products, such as computers and office automation equipment, takes place during this task.

Significant liaison with hardware and software vendors will have taken place at appropriate times.

2 Data Design

The data model is mapped onto a logical database or file design, taking into account the structuring rules of the DBMS or file access methods to be used. A physical design can then be proposed, taking into account the frequency of access of record types, type of access required and so on.

The design is progressively adjusted to produce a solution which provides an acceptable balance between performance and design durability. Various techniques have been developed to assess the performance of the design. The physical design can only be finalized after the program design work has been completed.

3 Program Design

The data processing (DP) facility required to support user-functions, e.g. conversational transaction, batch reports and personal computing facilities, has been decided in the User Design phase. The dialogues, inputs, outputs and processing algorithms have also been specified in detail. This task involves first of all partitioning the system into programs. The simplest solution is where one program supports one user-function. In some cases however the relationship is more complex.

After defining the function of each of these programs, the structure of the program is designed and the processing of each structural unit specified. Use of a data dictionary to record validation rules and processing algorithms during earlier phases will reduce the amount of writing to be done at this stage. A number of techniques are available to partition the system into programs and to design the programs. Where software packages are used, this task may be minimal or non-existent for those DP facilities to be provided by the packages.

4 Technical Transition Design

This task involves the technical design of conversion from the existing method of operation to the full use of the new system. Conversion and interface programs must be designed in the same way as in task 3. Programs may be needed for once-off conversion of files into the format required by the new system. Other programs will be needed to pass data to, or collect data from existing computer applications on a regular basis. In cases where data is not held on computer-readable files, procedures must be designed to gather and validate the data.

The design of a testing and training environment for the subsequent implementation is performed as part of this task. This includes the specification of testing and training files and the software characteristics required, e.g. diagnostic facilities. Procedures for the acceptance and take-on of new operational facilities should also be specified.

This task goes as far as designing not only the initial take-on of the new system, but its migration to eventual steady state running. In situations where the data is being taken on over a period of time, transition design may include file reorganization as quantities of data and access patterns change.

5 Operational Design

This task involves the drafting of:

- procedures for operating the mainframe and network, this includes recovery procedures, security controls, housekeeping tasks and end-user liaison
- operating instructions for batch jobs
- performance-monitoring procedures.

6 Sizing

This task follows the previous tasks and concerns the estimation of system performance and machine resource utilization. These estimates will have been performed at higher levels in previous stages, but during the Technical Design phase a high level of confidence should be achieved, e.g. within 5% of the calculation.

This includes elements of performance and resource utilization to be calculated and should include the following, which are not necessarily exhaustive:

- online response times and batch run times
- system availability estimates and recovery times
- filestore and mainstore estimates
- processor, storage media and communications network resource utilizations
- estimates of rates of change of the above.

7 Evaluation of Technical Design

The performance of the system has already been evaluated in task 2. This task concerns the re-appraisal of the costs of the remaining development work and the operational costs. The cost estimates should now be much more realistic. The revised development plan is produced. Any revisions to the prerequisites such as the User Design Specification, must be agreed and documented.

10.10 Major Product Descriptions

10.10.1 Technical Design Specification

Detail system design

This sets out the software and hardware environment within which the programs will run. Examples include the network design and arrangement of software to be used in the mainframe.

Flow diagrams of system and application architecture

This is a high level summary of the system specification and will include system flowcharts and network diagrams.

Database and file design

This specifies the complete definition of the system data storage and interface structures at logical and physical levels. Examples include file/database definitions and interfaces such as parameters.

Program specifications

This specifies the complete processing definition of the system. Examples include definitions of application, interface, housekeeping and 'middleware' programs; and of changes to these.

10.10.2 Revised Development Plan

This contains the latest refinements to cost, time-scale and resource requirement estimates for the rest of the system development. It will represent the latest state of knowledge about the future development of the system, including conversion/transition plans.

10.10.3 Revisions to Prerequisites

These revisions represent possible branches back into previous stages of system development and should be documented such that all revisions are justified and their impact on associated areas estimated.

10.10.4 Operating Procedures and Instructions

This is effectively a user manual for the operations department and should document exactly how the system is to be run, including areas where performance, etc. is to be monitored. Clear indication should be given on where liaison with other departments or sections is required.

10.11 Resources

The project team, consisting of:

- project leader, system designers and senior programmers, who should be supported by
- communications specialists, hardware specialists, systems programmers, computer operations staff and accountants.

10.12 Techniques and Tools

The tools used throughout this stage include data dictionaries, computer-aided software design packages, automatic file-design packages, application control and management systems, database management systems, query languages, application generators, sizing packages, and costing and planning packages.

We describe other techniques and tools under each task.

Task 1 Hardware and software configuration. The use of modelling techniques will be very useful at this stage for estimating hardware requirements.

Task 2 Data design. This stage requires the use of such techniques as software system sizing to provide the quantified justifications upon which design decisions will be based. The results of some of these sizing calculations will feed back into task 1.

Task 3 Program design. Techniques used during this stage include functional decomposition to decide on the optimum program network structure to give acceptable performance and maintainability. Structured program design techniques will be used to develop programs that are flexible and robust.

Task 4 Technical transition design. As this is a system within a system, techniques from the other tasks are likely to be involved here.

Task 5 Operational design. The techniques used here will include designing automated procedures to reduce errors, and the use of certain performance calculations for monitoring purposes.

Task 6 Sizing. Sizing techniques and numerical products will be useful during this task in order to speed up calculation and facilitate 'what if' queries.

Task 7 This is essentially an administrative task and involves costing and planning techniques, together with the use of documentation standards.

10.13 General Comments

The availability of sets of fourth generation software products should:

- reduce the costs and time to design and implement complex information systems
- help with control and maintenance during use
- make even more complex ideas feasible, include an integrated set of systems for:
    - data dictionary
    - application control and management
    - database management - relational and/or network
    - query language, retrieval
    - terminal and communications management.

At the other extreme, the availability of cheap microcomputers and cheap general-purpose information-handling software for word processing and fast searching of fairly simple records makes feasible the technical design and implementation of systems for very small organizations, or even one-person information systems.

10.14 References and Sources

None other than general references in Appendix 3.

10.15 Project Control

None.

10.16 Ideas and Suggestions

- Are any of the following problems and issues: communications infrastructure, human-computer interfaces, database, query languages, 4GLs, 5GLs, software engineering, AI, IKBS, administration, VLSI, liaison with others, how to demonstrate, how to build, how to co-ordinate, CAD/CAM, robotics, implementation?
- What techniques and tools are available?
- Which techniques and tools are appropriate?

V REVIEW AND CONTROL

11 REVIEW AND CONTROL

11.1 Extra Activities

You may find it helpful for us to classify in various ways the activities involved in the review and control of actions.

As you know, our framework structure has several levels of action:

- development
- phase
- task
- activity.

For clarity within this section we shall discuss the review and control of a 'task', though in general the word 'task' can be replaced by any of 'project', 'development', 'phase' or 'activity'. This frees us to use, in a new way, the words 'activity' and 'phase' to stand for the correct term for smaller and larger actions than the 'task' being reviewed and controlled.

In Chapter 2 we divided up the management cycle for a task into:

- planning it
- doing it
- reviewing and controlling it.

The review and control involves, as we explained in Section 2.4:

- extra activities *during* the period when the task is being done, e.g. to monitor the progress to date and to decide something about a current activity within the task
- extra activities *after* it has been done, e.g. to produce a progress report on completion.

These extra activities can also be classified into:

- activities that are *internal to the team* involved in the task, e.g. to ensure coordination
- activities that involve *external people*, e.g. to evaluate the deliverables and progress, and to relate them more widely, e.g. to the phase and development.

Generally these extra activities for review and control must be planned and done using far less time and resources than doing the task itself. Otherwise too much of the organization's total resources will be wasted on control. People will then feel that Big Brother is watching them too much, and that the overstaffed management is a waste

These extra activities involve **leadership**. The team leader must ensure that everyone in the team pulls their weight - doing the right activities well and as planned and scheduled. The team leader must continually make decisions about ongoing activities, so human relations skills are important. Respect, integrity and confidence can inspire others to perform well: their reward being recognition of achievement and esteem, not just their regular salary payment.

This book is not the place for an essay on leadership, but you may for the moment accept that:

- by and large you, and others at the tiller in your organization or controlling an information system task, are as good as similar people in other organizations

- you can learn from other people's experience, and this can apply in the area of review and control

- there is extensive experience in many industries of methods of management, including successful review and control

- computer-based information systems have existed long enough for such methods to be adapted and successfully applied to their development.

The activities involved in the review and control of a task vary in ways that make them difficult to list. Indeed attempting to list them may not help you. Certain types of activity, e.g. arranging regular meetings with papers and minutes, are appropriate for large long tasks taking months or years, but not for short tasks. So in this chapter we describe some of the concepts and techniques of review and control, without trying to formalize them into lists of activities and products. The leader of any particular task must decide which concepts and techniques are appropriate for a particular task in a particular environment and organization at a particular time. Generally the leader must lead, review and control the team by the internally oriented activities. But equally importantly he or she must arrange review and control activities that relate externally, e.g. to people involved in the phase or development, to people such as end-user representatives, and to people such as managers in the organization.

143

11.2 Review and Control Loop

One of the main reasons for drawing up a plan is to provide a basis for measuring progress. This means being able:

- to pinpoint problems
- to take avoiding action, because prevention is often better than cure
- to use management by exception, because highlighting the relevant information helps one concentrate on it
- to control the interactions between tasks
- to use techniques for monitoring progress.

The measurement of progress, including evaluation of current products, is used to make decisions that control future actions such as how the rest of the current task is done.

In general, the review and control can be viewed as a loop, as in Figure 11.1 which is a diagram of a basic model of control.

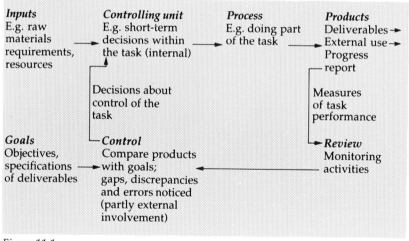

Figure 11.1

External people, e.g. representatives both of end-users and of the management of the wider phase or development, review and control, have their own work responsibilities and priorities. So they do not want to have to devote too much time to the review and control of other actions. Thus for successful larger tasks the feedback and control cycle may be formalized. The basic control model can be worked in two ways, or a combination of them, to achieve quality assurance from feedback.

144

Open-loop Control

This is effective where the relations between the inputs or control
variables and the outputs are known. Human beings often learn these
relationships and can anticipate the effects of changes in the input
conditions. Thus such people can decide what changes to make of the
controlling unit activity in order to produce an agreed desired change in
a deliverable. For example this may apply when the process of doing the
part of the task is automated.

Closed-loop, i.e. Feedback Control

This is more effective where the relationships are not clearly understood,
or where unpredictable changes occur in the system or in the system's
environment.

A discrepancy between the goal of the system and the system
performance must be detected in a feedback system before control action
can be started.

The time relationships in a system are very important in determining
control performance. The rate at which the system can change and the
lag or delay in feedback and corrective action are crucial parameters.

Continuous detection and feedback of the output may not be possible
and sampling is then used. Sampling, however, can then introduce delay.

11.3 Milestones

The leader may create in the plan for a task events that will be achieved
at regular intervals throughout doing the task and whose achievement
can be demonstrated. The selection of suitable events involves the
following.

- genuine steps towards the end-product indicate good progress
- events should be entered in the top-level plan
- the frequency should be appropriate
- presentations may be needed
- **milestones** should be total-system steps.

Each **milestone** may have the following contents:

- description of milestone
- system components
- testing level:
  - functional tests

- • performance measurements
- • reliability measurements
- documentation and support
- demonstration.

11.4 Reviews and Quality

For the project manager (or leader of a 'task') to be able to control a project (or 'task'), he or she must have up-to-date information on the current state of progress. This may be shown as:

- time reports
- histograms
- time graphs
- slip charts
- alert documents
- diaries
- cross-checks.

Regular control activities should involve the minimum number of people at any one time. Regular meetings scheduled with plenty of notice help ensure that the appropriate people are present. You are probably familiar with meetings that have an agenda of minutes, matters arising, correspondence, main items, any other business. But information system development can be reviewed and controlled by other styles of meeting. People sometimes like a change. We suggest also:

- quality assurance and control, e.g. by:
  - • walkthroughs
  - • inspections
  - • quality circles
- audit teams.

Quality Assurance and Control

Quality assurance is the function of setting and maintaining appropriate quality standards. It embraces all stages of product design and production and its function is to ensure that quality aspects are properly considered throughout development and production.

Quality control is concerned with maintaining the prescribed level of quality through testing and inspection.

There is now a general awareness of the need for equivalent quality assurance and quality control functions in the information-system development area. Most information-system development methodologies and project management systems contain elements of these based on:

- walkthroughs
- inspection techniques
- quality circles.

Walkthroughs

These are formal or semi-formal review sessions where a designer, coder or tester presents his work and justifies his decisions to the rest of a peer review team for the purpose of detecting errors. The leader may consider:

- types of walkthroughs
- programming teams
- roles in a walkthrough
- activities before, during and after a walkthrough
- psychology of walkthroughs
- management's role in walkthroughs.

Inspections

The inspection technique is an attempt to introduce the discipline of engineering into software development. The inspection process is highly formalized and it is carried out by a team, usually about four people, selected from outside the originators of the work being reviewed. Each team member has a well-defined role and the leader is suitably trained in advance.

The inspection process is divided into five stages:

- overview
- preparation
- meeting
- rework
- follow-up.

Quality Circles

A **Quality Circle** is a small group of people who do similar work and who meet together regularly, usually under the leadership of their supervisor and maybe on a voluntary basis, to:

- identify problems

- analyse the causes
- recommend solutions
- implement the solutions themselves.

For successful implementation of Quality Circles there are several considerations to be taken into account:

- steering committee
- facilitator
- circle leader
- circle members
- non-circle members
- management and specialists.

Audit Team

An audit team is usually a separate group from those doing the work. The **audit team** checks that procedures (such as the activities of the 'task') have been carried out satisfactorily and checks whether both deliverables and progress reports such as accounts are correct. They may invent activities to test the procedures, for example producing extra listings from a data dictionary, and testing a deliverable system on data and commands representing a situation that they invent.

11.5 How To

It is impossible for us to describe project management activities, but a leader should think about:

- how to organize a project from beginning to end
- how to structure a plan that stands up under pressure
- how to get people to accept and participate in your plans
- how to set measurable project objectives
- how to motivate team members when the job gets tough
- how to help team members solve their own problems
- how best to utilize available resources
- how to cut out waste of time and money
- how to measure project performance
- how to use information systems that can respond to project needs.

11.6 Problems and Pitfalls

Both the parent organization as a whole and the project (i.e. 'task') team must employ project managerial techniques to ensure that judicious and adequate use is made of the planning, controlling and communications systems. These management techniques must include preparation, such as:

- clearly established specifications and designs
- realistic schedules
- realistic cost estimates
- avoidance of buy-ins
- avoidance of over-optimism
- developing clear understandings of the relative importance of cost, schedule and technical performance goals.

Major causes for the failure of project management in information-system development include:

- selecting a concept which was not applicable
- the wrong person selected as project manager
- upper management not supportive
- inadequately defined tasks
- management techniques misused
- project termination not planned.

This implies the following management pitfalls:

- lack of planning
- lack of self-control - i.e. not knowing oneself
- activity traps
- managing versus doing
- people versus task skills
- ineffective communications
- time management
- management bottlenecks.

Projects should be established with objectives in mind. Project objectives must be:

- specific, not general
- not overly complex
- measurable, tangible and verifiable
- realistic and attainable

- established within resource bounds
- consistent with resources available or anticipated
- consistent with organizational plans, policies and procedures.

11.7 Conflicts

Conflicts in the control of a project (or task) can arise from the following potential sources:
- conflict over project priorities
- conflict over administrative procedures
- conflict over technical opinions and performance trade-offs
- conflict over manpower resources
- conflict over cost
- conflict over schedules
- personality conflict.

Modes of handling a conflict include:

- withdrawal
- smoothing
- compromising
- forcing
- confrontation.

We have adapted the following table from [THAM75]. It gives the relative placing of the intensity of conflicts from various types of source at various stages of a project life-cycle. The values 1 to 3 indicate the likeliest sources of conflict.

Phase:	Formulation of project	Planning and build-up of project	Doing the main programme	Phase out
Source of conflict				
Project priorities	1	1	4	4
Administrative procedures	2	3	5	7
Schedules	3	2	1	1
Manpower	4	5	3	3
Cost	5	7	6	5
Technical problems	6	4	2	6
Personalities	7	6	7	2

11.14 References and Sources

ARCH76: Archibald, R.D. *Managing High-Technology Programs and Projects* John Wiley (1976).

AVOT69: Avots, I. Why Does Project Management Fail? *California Management Review* Vol. 12 (1969) 77-82.

BUCK77: Buckle, J.K. *Managing Software Projects*. Macdonald and Janes (1977).

GILB77: Gilb, T. *Software Metrics*. Winthrop (1977).

HODG68: Hodgetts, R.M. Leadership Techniques in Project Organizations. *Academy of Management Journal* Vol. 11 (1968) 211-219.

KERZ79: Kerzner, H. *Project Management: A Systems Approach to Planning, Scheduling and Controlling*. Van Nostrand Reinhold (1979).

KILL71: Killian, W.P. Project Management - Future Organizational Concepts. Marquette *Business Review* No. 2 (1971) 90-107.

MORL81: Morland, J. *Quality Circles*. The Industrial Society (1981).

THAM75: Thamhain, H.J. & Wilemon, D.L. Conflict Management in Project Life Cycles. *Sloan Management Review* (Summer 1975) 31-50.

WEIN71: Weinberg, G.M. *The Psychology of Computer Programming*. Van Nostrand Reinhold (1971).

WILE70: Wilemon, D.L. & Cicero, J.P. The Project Manager: Anomalies and Ambiguities. *Academy of Management Journal* Vol. 13 (1970) 269-282.

YOUR79: Yourdon, E.N. *Structured Walkthroughs*. Prentice Hall (1979).

11.16 Ideas and Suggestions

- Does your organization have a strategy and tactics for implementing total quality?
- What about Just In Time (JIT)?
- Do you have appropriate actions in your area of your organization?
- Manufacturing or service organizations spend about 20% of sales revenue on costs that relate to quality. This includes waste of material, efforts and costs of goodwill.
- Do you regard it as failure to deliver equally to being late, if an exact date and time has been agreed?
- What actions do you take on various kinds of feedback?

- What would you do if profits in your area were too low or cost 10 percent too high?
- How could you improve your customer's satisfaction - and how do you measure that?
- Are performance and feedback on low level operations good? Could anyone who phones you ever be left hanging on the phone for ages? How do you know?
- Do you collect quality data at key places in your area?
- Do you fully understand the appropriate statistical techniques?
- Do you use standard computer software packages that are available for these tasks?

VI CONCLUSION

12 LOOKING BACK AND LOOKING FORWARD

This book establishes a framework for the management, planning, control, analysis, design, implementation and maintenance of information systems. This framework provides a basis for effective information systems development. It may be used as a template for systems project management and control: within it contemporary development methods and methodologies may be employed. It stands as a statement of all the elements that may be required during information systems analysis and design. It offers scope for analogy, temptation to learn, reminders to the forgetful and the means by which new ideas and their pursuance may be judged.

This chapter deals with applicability of the framework, principal issues which concerned the group, and key points which have evolved from the discussion.

12.1 Applicability

We never consciously decided to limit our work to certain types of projects. Theories, methodologies, techniques and tools were considered. Where they did not fit the framework it was modified.

While judgement of the value of this work is in its relevance to the practical, we believe the framework to be applicable to all types of information systems work, including:

1   large, global, medium and small projects

2   computer systems and the manual aspects of computer-based information systems

3   simple and complex applications or combinations of applications

4   mainframes, computers, minicomputers, microcomputers, word processors and other information-engineering products

5   package based and bespoke solutions

6   centralized or distributed solutions

7   different applications, such as
    • transaction processing systems
    • management information systems, decision support systems

- intelligent knowledge-based systems, expert systems
- office automation systems.

8   different development approaches, such as
  - life-cycle
  - evolutionary
  - incremental
  - prototyping
  - parallel.

12.2 Describing the Framework for Development Approaches

The issue of whether to adapt the straightforward 'life-cycle' approach to systems development probably occupied us more than any other topic.

During the 1960s and 1970s some people applied the so-called life-cycle approach to the development of information systems in commerce.

At first in our internal working papers some of us used such a development framework with phases and with decision points between them. But this was repeatedly questioned as the work proceeded, in favour of the framework described in Chapter 2 that pays more attention to the need for early partial systems, and other assumptions discussed below.

Various pressures have caused systems professionals to consider alternative methods of development.

Increasing demand for systems is causing many people to look for ways to improve productivity so that systems can be developed more quickly. This is being made possible by the increasing availability of the so-called *fourth generation languages* such as MANTIS, UFO and FOCUS which enable applications to be generated in far less time then using traditional programming languages.

New types of end-users are being encountered. Before long most organizations will have computerized their basic transaction processing systems. Instead they will be looking at the information needs of middle and upper management and at the same time thinking of ways in which technology can be of assistance to them, for example, through the provision of *office automation* equipment. Organizations which are already looking at the needs of management are running up against several problems when trying to apply traditional development methods.

- Many managers and user representatives find it hard to define their precise needs.

154

- Their requirements continually change - especially as the business environment changes.
- They are incredibly busy and are loath to spend vast amounts of time talking to systems people and reading reports prepared by systems people.

New sets of problems are being encountered for which there is no off-the-shelf solution. Developers have had considerable practice over the past years developing transaction-processing systems. But few people have developed management information systems, office automation systems, decision support systems or expert systems.

Some methodologies differ from the life-cycle approach in that they involve repetition, by repeating the life-cycle or parts of it. Sometimes some of the stages are combined, and programs are developed gradually by adding features [MADD59]. Essentially, over perhaps many months, the developers always have a working program or system, but each day they add to it.

The prototype approach is based on repeated execution of the life-cycle phases with increasing detail, thus progressing towards final acceptance by the user. A **prototype** means a first type or model from which later improved copies will be made. The prototype will be discarded, e.g. if reprogrammed in a different language for better implementation. The prototype approach is justified as a cheap trial development of particular features. But nowadays *prototype* is also used to mean developing gradually as in the previous paragraph.

Some people use the terms **evolutionary** or **incremental** to mean building a system by creating a small part, e.g. the core, and adding bit by bit.

Provided the project manager and the relevant other project team members have the understanding and rare ability to analyse and synthesize correctly at the highest levels of abstraction, it is possible for example to:

- do the relevant data analysis and functional analysis for part of the users' requirements, e.g. develop a local model for an area
- do the corresponding part of user design
- do a small corresponding technical design
- implement a system for part of one corresponding application, like a prototype for demonstration and discussion, using a database management system to make implementation easy
- gradually extend by appropriate further analysis and design, i.e. incrementally add features and facilities.

However, for success, the project manager and team must so fully understand data analysis and the facilities of their database management systems (DBMS) and other software that they are confident that they cannot run into problems as they analyse other local areas for other applications, merge the local models, create global models of increasing complexity and correspondingly extend their implementation. For example with an entity-attribute-relationship (EAR) conceptual model various problems can arise in splitting entity types, in introducing further entity types to accommodate attributes of relationships, from candidate identifiers in later local models, and from inaccurate normalization. These problems may lead to splitting or joining relations in an implemented relational model, or in a Codasyl-based model to splitting record types and set types in ways for which existing DBMSs do not have facilities.

On the other hand, DBMSs with good facilities for logical and physical data independence; impact analysis; unloading, restructuring and reloading; and ensuring consistency, may successfully be used. For example new applications using existing data types may be added without affecting existing application programs. New record types, relationships and data items may be added. The physical storage structure may be changed as the pattern of use changes. Analysts, designers and programmers may find it easier to think out how to add a new application facility to existing coding for a complex system than they or end-users would find writing a complete specification for the complex system including the extra facility before any part is implemented.

Of course the arrival of alternative development approaches presents planners and management with a different problem - *how to select the most appropriate approach*. We do not necessarily have the answer, but one way of deciding may be to try to match the type of system being developed with the most appropriate development approach by drawing up a list of the pros and cons of the various approaches for the proposed information system.

For example, arguably the best approach to developing a transaction processing system with easily identified requirements is the life-cycle approach. On the other hand, a decision support system will most likely change over the development period of early use as each manager's appreciation of the information requirements and IS facilities become clearer through the discussion and use of the system. For this situation the incremental approach might be more suitable.

After discussion we internally agreed for purposes of description to adopt phases, because to do so is traditional and widely understood and all tasks must be placed within some structure.

We then also agreed:

- that the structure of the scheduling of phases and tasks should be through prerequisites and products
- that later phases and tasks could start as soon as primitive versions of its prerequisites were available as primitive versions of the products of earlier phases and tasks
- that the earlier phases and tasks could continue concurrently with the phases and tasks started later, with feedback and incremental improvement of all primitive products
- that the phases such as analysis and design should be describable in internal working papers using the 15 sub-sections that most of the chapters have.

The framework of BSP, ISSP, ISTP and ISPP evolved as those four named types of planning gradually. A phase about 'Global Design', i.e. organization-wide design decisions, was dropped. Extensive problems of incompleteness and inconsistency among tasks, products and terms remained.

Taking the medicine we recommend, the editor resolved these by a mixture of incremental and parallel development, in many places rewriting the internal working paper drafts, and using a data dictionary system [MADD84] to hold a draft version of the index and check for certain kinds of consistency.

12.3 Management

The problem with treating management in the book was whether to incorporate the planning, review and control aspects within the phases as separate tasks or as parallel tasks. Strict planning was made a separate topic. Management review and control were combined.

We believe that the role of management and the tasks of planning, review and control are at the very hub of successful systems development.

There is a considerable need for the top management of the organization,whatever its size, to be involved in the provision of information systems.

Top management, at board level or equivalent, should be aware of the importance of the information systems to the achievement of the business objectives.

The increase in perceived importance of exercises such as corporate data analysis is helping to improve the situation. However management at the highest level should also maintain their involvement during the development, in order to provide the weight of authority that may become necessary.

In the current environment of cost consciousness and performance indicators, the need to plan the optimum use of resources, particularly people, is generally recognized. Less well recognized, but of equal importance, is the need for effective review and control, in order to keep the project in line with the objectives. Many of the project problems, particularly technical ones, may be prevented or reduced in impact by more effective management.

12.4 Task Dependencies

Our detailed phase and task descriptions in this book include products and prerequisites at each stage. Each action depends on others.

This emphasis on the dependencies is at the heart of successful systems development, providing triggers for management control and intermediate objectives for the technical work.

The checking of prerequisites against current products provides a measurable indicator of progress and quality. It provides a basis for milestones and management checkpoints.

If the development runs into problems, then tracing back through the prerequisites can provide a controlled way of 'looping back' in order to bring the project back into line. The further back the re-iteration has to be done, then the higher the problem can be escalated, as more fundamental statements may be questioned.

12.5 Complete Checklist

The detailed task descriptions, together with their products, prerequisites and interfaces, provide a skeleton and checklist for information system development planning, together with appropriate management. This provides the meat of the book.

The tasks and activities probably represent a superset of that required for any one project. However, if the descriptions are reviewed and the necessary tasks are identified then two benefits accrue.

1   A checklist is then obtained, which may be put into the project plan to ensure that all necessary work is done, at the right time. Tasks which are omitted are more likely to be so because they cannot be justified, rather than because they have been forgotten.

2   For the chosen tasks, the required resources effort, skills, tools and techniques may be estimated and the detailed project plan established.

12.14 References and Sources

MADD59: R.N. Maddison. *Commercial Applications of Computers.* Thesis. Oxford (1959).

MADD84: R.N. Maddison & A.J. Gawronski. A Data Dictionary for Learning Data Analysis. (DADICS) *Computer J.* Vol 28 No 3 (July 1985) p270-281.

APPENDIX 1

OUR TERMS OF REFERENCE

1.1 Background

We, the authors of this book, came together through personal contact - some of us had known each other professionally for many years. We created our own terms of reference.

Our aims were to research, discuss and document what work should be done to develop information systems successfully, perhaps concentrating more on techniques for planning, strategy analysis and design. Techniques for implementation, system building, maintenance, use, testing and removal might be omitted or played down. We also wanted to concentrate on issues relevant to management for success.

1.2 Terms of Reference

1.2.1 Objectives

Our self-prescribed Terms of Reference included the following objectives:

- to develop and document a framework which should be applied to the development of computer-based information systems. The framework arrived at should, as far as possible, be:
  - practical, and independent of the size and complexity of the system
  - independent of any proprietary tools or techniques
  - applicable for the next ten years
- to identify the various design techniques, development aids and documentation tools whose use should be considered in the planning, analysis and design of information systems
- to determine the way in which identified techniques and tools may be used together during the systems development process to facilitate the planning, analysis and design of information systems
- to complete the whole and produce a book within two and a half years
- to have regular meetings, with circulated draft papers.

Careful attention was to be given to the problems which face current systems designers and the various development approaches which are being discussed at the moment, including:

- life-cycle
- incremental
- prototyping
- user development of systems
- evolutionary development.

We also intended to update the book in future years if circumstances justified that.

1.2.2 Scope

It was agreed that we would initially consider the entire development process from initial conception through to the implementation of a production system, in order to define a comprehensive systems development framework. Once such a framework had been documented and agreed, we would concentrate on the planning, analysis and design activities. By narrowing the scope in this way, it was hoped that we would be able to achieve a meaningful set of results in two and half years.

APPENDIX 2

GLOSSARY OF INFORMATION SYSTEM TERMS

To IS specialists or others a term herein may have a special meaning - with connotations slightly different from the natural English language meaning. Thus for some terms we distinguish:

- (ENL) English Natural Language meaning - e.g. as in an English dictionary
- (IS) Information Systems specialists meaning
- (AI) meaning among Artificial Intelligence researchers
- (GST) meaning within General Systems Theory
- (CS) meaning as in Computer Science
- (Math) Mathematical meaning
- (T) Technical or technology meaning

Many terms can have 'type' or 'class' added: e.g. 'entity', 'entity type', 'entity class'. The terms 'entity type' and 'entity class' mean a collection or set of entity occurrences that are similar. In written text and speech the word 'type' or 'class' is often dropped, e.g. where no confusion should arise and the context should imply whether an entity occurrence or an entity type is being discussed. Generally an 'entity type' (or ' ... type') means a *named* class of 'entity' (or '...') occurrences.

Different meanings are either numbered to clarify the end of one meaning from the start of another, or start with one of (ENL), (IS) , (AI), (GST),... or are separated by | . The notation | ... means other meanings (usually in ENL) omitted.

The notation 'accuracy-IS2' means accuracy with its IS2 meaning.

Abstract: (ENL1) to summarize. (ENL2) to separate by the operation of the mind - as in forming a general mental concept from considering particular occurrences. (ENL3) denoting the quality, condition, attribute or association of a thing apart from the thing itself - e.g. 'hardness'. (IS) as ENL 2.

Abstract machine: (CS) theoretical or mathematical model of a computer, e.g. for formalizing algorithms, discussing compatibility, programming.

Abstraction: (ENL) to draw away | summarize | separate by operation of the mind. (Math) The process of separating form (= structure) from content (= values); i.e. going from instances to the rule for the general case.

Access: (ENL) admittance | opportunity of approach or entry | way or route.

Access control: (IS) mechanism ensuring who and what is allowed what access to what - e.g. by doors with keys or software checks.

Access mode: (IS) class of access; e.g. retrieve, update, execute, use in a given process.

Access path: (IS1) method of finding information or data, e.g. from its association with some quotable key, e.g. 'the software provides a direct access path to the record for student A1234567'.
(IS2) method of finding further data, e.g. from its association with data already found, e.g. can access that student's courses and tutors records.

Access path analysis: (IS) analysis concentrating on access path types.

Access right: (IS) conceptual model of privacy, e.g. who has the right to access what data in what access mode.

Access time: (IS& CS) time taken to retrieve, copy or update stored data, e.g. time for disk transfers/total time to transmit command from terminal to remote computer, retrieve required data and get reply back, as seen by end-user.

Accuracy, accurate: (ENL) correctness, exactness.
(Math) no difference between true value and calculated value.
(T) no difference between true values and measured value.
(IS1) agreement with relevant part of the real world (RW).
(IS2) agreement assuming end-users' transactions are correct.

Act: (ENL) to do something | to exert force or influence | to behave | ...
(AI) an event-AI with an animate agent-AI.

Action: (ENL) activity | behaviour | deed | operation | mechanism , e.g. of keyboard, equipment | ...
(IS1) action (as ENL) of person or equipment, e.g. action of end-user. (IS2) retrieval or update operation on an information base.
(IS3) elementary (= atomic) subprocess that has some explicit result | group of such subprocesses that together yield a result.

Activity: (T & IS) action, taking time and resources, as in PERT or CPA (Programme Evaluation and Review Technique, Critical Path Analysis), e.g. 'build east wall', 'test system'.

(IS2) group of actions or task, usually associated with a particular business function in an organization, e.g. 'process sales order 1234'.

Activity type: (IS) named class of similar activities-IS2, e.g. 'process sales order'.

Actor: (ENL& IS) one who acts. (AI) one type of active element in a conceptual graph (the other types being: function, transaction), e.g. actors pass messages.

Actual: (ENL& IS1) real, existing in fact.
(IS2) as in the relevant 'real world': as opposed to the things that might have been but didn't exist, i.e. allowable in the universe of discourse.

Agent: (ENL) a person or thing that acts, or that exerts power, or causes something to happen | someone authorized or delegated to act on behalf of someone else |... (AI) the relation linking an act-AI to an animate actor-AI.

Aggregate: (ENL) to collect into a whole | to assemble | formed or parts that combine into a whole (IS) named collection of e.g. attributes, data items; e.g. 'Date' is an aggregate of Year, Month, Day.

Aggregate entity type: (IS) named entity type in 3NF or 4NF or 5NF with full identifier shown. All the non-identifying attributes are fully functionally dependent on the identifier; the aggregate may be created by collecting together such attributes according to what each attribute is fully functionally dependent on.

Aggregate model: (IS) CDM like EAR model but with each entity type shown as an aggregate entity type; the attributes being grouped together according to what they are functionally dependent on.

Aim: (ENL) general statement of intention, direction |...

Allowable: could have happened | existed in the relevant real world, i.e. may or may not have actually (see UOD).

Amend: (ENL) to correct, improve, rectify, make better | ... (IS) to change the value of an occurrence | to change stored data representing a fact.

Analyse: to subject to analysis.

Analysis: (ENL) resolving or separating something into its parts | ...

Analysis phase: (IS) the phase or stage of IS development during which analysis is done.

Analyst: (ENL) person skilled at analysis-ENL. (IS1) role of doing analysis. (IS2) person skilled in doing such. (IS3) job title of person doing planning, analysis, design in ISD generally.

164

Animate: (ENL) to give life to I to enliven I to actuate I moving as if alive I ...

Application: (ENL) the act of applying or using I a thing applied I .... (IS) transaction and / or operation, e.g. 'change of address', 'payroll'.

Application program: (IS& CS) program for servicing a particular type of transaction, e.g. to update stored addresses at each change of address.

Application type: (IS) class of similar transactions and operations, e.g. apparently serviced by one program, using different data for each occurrence.

Approximate: here means to make a judgement of the order of magnitude of a system project. The judgement is based on personal experience and knowledge of the general area. Approximations are less precise than estimates.

Atomic: (Chemistry) pertaining to atoms - atoms (in older chemistry) being so small that they cannot be cut or subdivided I ...
(IS& CS) not meaningfully broken into finer structure, i.e. further analysis is not relevant or useful.

Attribute: (ENL, IS & AI) property, quality or quantity assigned to or associated with an object or entity, e.g. '1983'. An attribute may be optional, e.g. some people have a telephone number, some don't.

Attribute type: (IS) named recognized class of similar attribute occurrences, e.g. 'Year-of-birth'. Equivalently a type of quality or quantity for which each occurrence of a particular entity type has or may have a value, e.g. each Person has a Year-of-birth.

Attribute-value pair: (IS) a named attribute type and an occurrence of its value e.g. 'Date of order' is '7 Jan 1987'.

Behaviour: (ENL) conduct I ... (behaviour is changeable, personality is not). (GST) collection of possible system states and changes. (IS) dynamics of a (target) system.

Building: (CS) tying of a software process to a data structure, usually for efficiency and irreversible, e.g. an application program is linked to a particular subschema of a particular database schema for a run by a user.

Business event: typically something that happens outside of or inside an organization and that may or should influence what the organization does. A business event may be a regular occurrence, e.g. receipt of a customer's order, or an irregular occurrence, e.g. a change in VAT rates. A business event will trigger one or more activities and/or business functions.

Business function: (IS) class of activities proper to the organization's purpose, e.g. 'sales', 'sales order processing' | ... a meaningful unit of business work, as perceived by an-end-user of a system. Business functions may be analysed into lower-level units, also termed business function, to any useful number of levels.

Business function data model: represents a subset of the data described by the System Data Model. It describes information required to support a particular business function.

Candidate identifier: (IS1) possible identifying attribute type (or composite group of attributes) such that for each entity occurrence the attribute(s) have unique (distinct) values, e.g. National Insurance numbers or National Health Service numbers could identify employees, chassis numbers or Registration numbers could identify vehicles. (IS2) as IS1 but not selection as the preferred identifying attributes.

Cardinality: (ENL& IS) how many occur. (IS) cardinality of a relation means how many tuples.

Character: (ENL& IS) letter or symbol in writing | ...

Class: (ENL) a rank or order of things or persons, e.g. 'high class' | a scientific classification | to form methodically into a class or classes | ...
(Math1) collection of things (= the elements or members) with at least one common property.
(Math2) Equivalence class: a group of elements/members such as 'all Mondays' which satisfy a mathematical equivalence relation; all Tuesdays is another equivalence class occurrence; the class of all dates subdivides into seven such classes.

CODASYL: Conference on Data & System Languages, various years.

Command: (IS1) a message that requests action. (IS2) the identifying word or term in a command type, e.g. 'find', 'print'; usually the first word of a command and reserved for that meaning and use.

Communication: (ENL) a message that is sent and received. (IS) the passing of a message (e.g. data such as a string of symbols/signs) from an origin to a destination.

Composite: (IS& CS) collection of two or more of something, e.g. named attribute types, usually without having a name for the collection; e.g. 'Student-no, Course-no'.

Conceptual: (ENL) appertaining to a 'mental image', an idea formed in the mind. (IS) Same but especially appertaining to an analyst's, developer's or user's image of the 'real world' and concentrating on the meaning. Please distinguish:

166

(1) a 'real world' object or process, e.g. I threw a 6 with a particular dice at 7.20 pm on a particular date;
(2) the mental image that you have of that (you didn't see the dice);
(3) a representation as symbols, e.g. '1920: RNM threw 6'.

Conceptual data model CDM: the rules and structure of data that represents the types of information in the universe of discourse; i.e. the structure of data in a model that maps the relevant real world.

Conceptual model CM: a model describing the allowable (=UOD) objects, information, processes, flows and the interrelationships of these; e.g. what is used where, when, how and why. (The information and processes need not be computerized.)

Conceptual process model CPM: the rules and structure of the types of processes and flows, whether computerized or not.

Conceptual schema CS: an agreed central full description of all relevant information types, i.e. the necessary propositions covering the whole of the relevant part of an organization, the allowable universe of discourse, and resolving users' views before design of an implemented IS. Equivalently, a formal description of all rules and structure that apply to a UOD; a set of semantic rules - i.e. stating the meaning.
(IS2) The conceptual schema of a database means its fundamental structure, determining what data is allowed to be stored and what operations are allowed.

Concrete: (ENL& IS) denoting a physical real-world thing, not an attribute, quality or state.

Condition: (ENL) a state in which things exist | a state that restricts or limits something | ... (Math) that which must precede the application of a clause; e.g. in 'if (condition) then (clause)' where (condition) and (clause) are to be replaced appropriately. (IS& CS1) a testable state involving data; so that if the condition is true then a process is to be performed, e.g. if net-pay-before-tax > 0 then calculate-tax. (IS& CS2) see precondition and postcondition.

Connotation: (ENL) to signify secondarily, implying something more than the primary significance. The **denotation** of a word is its primary significance, e.g. as in a dictionary or glossary. A **connotation** is an associated feeling suggested to some people; e.g. 'home', 'family' have happier connotations than 'building', 'people'. Many IS terms have connotations.

Constraint: (ENL) loss of freedom of action | to restrict by an imposed condition. (AI, Math) a limit to the choice of expression or values.

Control: Organizational procedures to determine deviations from plans and initiate correct action. (IS) **Control model** of an organization means from the formulae in the model and from the data about the real world the IS provides for decision making.

Corporate data model: (IS) is initially formulated during strategic planning or at the start of a major design project involving multiple system phases that have not been preceded by a strategic planning phase. It must be simple and clear, in business terms, as it acts as the route map for determining the scope and inter-relationship of the more detailed data models based upon it.

Currency: (IS) In CODASYL-based DBMSs the record occurrences that have most recently been found or stored during the execution of the application program are the **current** records of various classes. The **currency** is the address of the current record.

Current: (IS) Catering only for the latest information, forgetting historical data, e.g. holding details of current patients but not records of past ones. (IS2) See Currency.

Data: (ENL) facts given, from which others may be deduced, inferred. (IS& CS) signs or symbols, especially as for transmission in communication systems and for processing in computer systems; usually but not always representing information, agreed facts or assumed knowledge; and represented using agreed characters, codes, syntax and structure.

Data administration: organization-wide coordination of information systems and standards.

Data aggregate: (IS& CS) named collection of data items, maybe part or all of a record type.

Data analysis: analysis and documentation of the structure of information types, e.g. as local and global CDMs leading to logical data models. The act of ensuring that a data resource is accurately, completely and consistently documented. It may be documented in a data dictionary.

Data assurance: (IS) responsibility for ensuring that stored data is accurate, up to date, secure, protected, consistent.

Data description: (IS1) processable representation of the names, structure and use of data types. (IS2) full descriptions, e.g. with text and diagrams for easy understanding.

Data description language DDL: processable language for data descriptions.

Data dictionary DD: (IS) repository for all meta information, e.g. about CDMs, CPMs, CS, logical models, SS, processes, programs; with sources, authors, dates, reasons.

Data dictionary system DDS: (IS) a computerized DD service, with facilities for queries, updates.

Data duplication: (IS) more than one occurrence of the same data item value, e.g. representing different information.

Data flow diagram DFD: (IS) diagram showing information flows between user activities or functional areas; see IFD.

Data independence: (IS) facilities in a DBMS to change independently, where consistent, any subschema, schema, storage schema, without attention to anything whose purpose is unaltered.

Data item: (IS& CS) occurrence of data, regarded as atomic; logical or physical.

Data item type: (IS& CS) named class of data items that occur.

Data manipulation language DML: (IS) language for programming updates, retrievals and other database operations.

Data model: (IS) a formalized description of the structure of the types of elements within a data resource.

Data redundancy: (IS) more than one logically occurring representation as data of a unit of information; maybe for efficiency or maybe undesirable; excluding backup copies.

Data resource: (IS) a major group of an organization's data, e.g. corresponding to a division of the organization's business.
Database: (IS):
1 a collection of data items structured to be used for many applications, with controlled redundancy.
2 as 1 controlled through a DBMS.
3 a collection of many such databases forming an information system.
4 such a collection representing information for a specific universe of discourse. Users need to distinguish what represents the actual real world from other allowable possibilities.

Database administrator DBA: administrator of database, DBMS and service to users, maybe including data assurance.

Database control system DBCS: the part of a DBMS usable during application program runs.

Database management system DBMS: software package for controlling databases, providing application program interfaces, performance monitoring, security, recovery, evolutionary use.

Degree of relation: (IS) how many named attribute types; i.e. how many domains and roles; i.e. how many columns.

Degree of relationship: (IS) rule of allowable cardinalities of association between occurrences of the two entity types; e.g. one to many.

Denotation: (ENL) The primary significance of a word (as in a dictionary or glossary). Compare connotation.

Descriptive: giving description for human understanding; e.g. descriptive attribute type.

Design: (ENL) a plan, outline, sketch, drawing of an intended product | ...

Designing: (ENL) the art or creative work of making designs.

Design phase: (IS) the work of fully specifying what is to be implemented, e.g. as the target IS. Compare analysis phase.

Diagram: a graphical or symbolic representation of certain features of something, needed for exposition.

Document: (ENL) paper giving information | ...
(IS) unit of recorded information, e.g. (until recently) printed by a computer system; with a suitable logical structure, tables, lists and text | the equivalent of such in any other form (e.g. displayed, or transmitted), not necessarily on paper.

Domain: (ENL) what territory one has dominion over | the scope or range of a subject or sphere of knowledge | ...
(Math & IS) the collection of values to which a mathematical mapping can be applied. A mathematical function is a mapping from one set of values (= the domain) to another set (= the codomain). An object (in the domain) maps to one or more image(s) (in the codomain). The collection of all actual images is called the **range**. e.g.: Sue dances Mon & Thurs, Jo dances Fri. Domain | = - {Sue, Jo}, codomain = {Mon, Tues,... Sun}, Range = {Mon, Thurs, Fri}, Image of Jo = Fri.
(Database) The named set of values that can occur in a column in relation (= table), e.g. Days-of-the-week | The named set of values that a data item can take.

Duplication: (IS) e.g. the name of an attribute type appearing more than once in a model.
(IS) e.g. the same value being stored more than once. E.g. suppose Customer orders may have a Delivery-address and an Account-address (two pieces of information) and these are held/modelled as two data

item types, then for orders where the two addresses are the same the address will be stored twice (= duplication). There is no redundancy here - both copies are needed to represent the two pieces of information.

Element. (ENL) a first principle | an essential part of something | ... (Chem) a substance that cannot be chemically resolved into simpler chemical substances. (Math) a member of a set. (IS) an atomic name, term or word.

End-user EU: (IS) anyone in the role of user of an IS; not developer or provider; issues messages, including commands, to the information system and receives messages from it.

Entity: (ENL) a thing that really exists (as opposed to its qualities and associations) | ...
(IS1) any concrete or abstract thing of interest, including an association among things. This means any thing in the universe of discourse, i.e. including things that might have existed or happened but did not.
(IS2) the denotation of a meaningful item of data, e.g. the house at the address given in the data item, or the person identified by a string of characters.

Entity attribute relationship model, EAR: (IS) model representation for CDMs with named entity, relationship and attribute types.

Entity identifier: (IS) The attribute or composite collection of attributes selected and preferred to identify and distinguish the occurrences of an entity type.

Entity life-cycle: (IS) creation, changes to, and end of existence of each entity occurrence; checking that all these are possible for all entity types.

Entity model: (IS) brief synonym for ER or EAR model.

Entity occurrence: (IS) same as entity-IS1 and -2, occurrence of an entity type.

Entity relationship model, ER: (IS) model like EAR but initially concentrating on entity types and relationship types, assuming attribute types may be added later.

Entity relationship attribute model, ERA: same as EAR.

Entity type: (IS1) named class of similar entities, especially in EAR, ER models, so each occurrence has the same attributes and does or may have the same relationships; usually derived or produced by analysis. (IS2) as IS1, but maybe artificial or normalized, so as to have some particular useful properties.

Entry point: (IS) a method by which an EU may specify which data occurrences are to be found not assuming any already found.

Environment: (ENL) and (IS1) surrounding conditions that influence growth and development. (IS2) the environment of an IS is that part of the real world that contains the end-users that exchange messages with the IS. (IS& Tech) appropriate or controlled temperature, humidity, cleanliness and so on around equipment and people.

Estimate: means to determine the costs and benefits of the next phase of systems development based on detailed work plans. Estimates imply a high degree of accuracy since there is substantial support backing them up; as opposed to approximations, which are judgements of the order of magnitude.

Event: (ENL) that which happens | an incident | ... (Planning) a logical node between activities; the start or finish point of an activity.
(IS) receipt of information or a time point; especially that may trigger activities or indicate the end of an activity | (widened to) any logical situation or time point of interest, e.g. an interruption, a change; the fact that something has happened, in the universe of discourse, the information system, or the environment. (GST) a state transition, i.e. change from one state to another. (AI) a collection of one or more acts by animate agents and/or happenings that do not involve agents.

Event analysis: (IS) means the identification of business and system events and the types of activities and functions which are triggered by an occurrence of each type of event.

Event type: a class of such events.

Exclusive relationships: (IS) each entity occurrence may belong to an occurrence of one or the other relationship type, but not both.

Existence condition: (IS) rule about entity occurrences.

External: outside whatever is to be modelled; arising from outside or partly.

External schema, ES: (IS) a view of data for a process for an application or end-user that is not among the providers of the IS.

Fact: sentence assumed or known to be true.

Feasibility study: work undertaken to determine whether computerization of a particular area is practical and cost-justified; or to decide between alternatives by evaluating which is the best possibility.

Fixed retention: (IS) a member record occurrence that has an owner through a relationship cannot change which relationship occurrence it belongs to.

Flow: (ENL) moving, e.g. running water | ... (IS) data or information moving.

Full functional dependency: (IS) an attribute is fully functionally dependent on others means all the others are needed.

Function: 1 business function; 2 mathematical function.

Functional area: (IS) that part of the organization responsible for a single business function.

Functional analysis: (IS) analysis oriented to business functions.

Functional decomposition: (IS) functional analysis done in steps of increasing detail.

Functional dependency: (Math & IS) an attribute is functionally dependent on others if quoting values for them implies which value of it corresponds.

Functional dependency analysis: (IS) analysis concentrating on the interdependence of business functions - nothing to do with functional dependency.

Functionality: (IS) what processes the system is capable of doing.

Global: covering the whole organization or universe of discourse, or the whole of the relevant part.

Global CDM: a global CDM may be derived by merging or extending local CDMs for areas.

Goal: the desired object of an activity involving effort or ambition. It may or may not be achievable.

Graphical representation: representation e.g. lines on paper where the intensity (darkness, brightness) of a line does not imply data, but the line position or connectivity does.

Graphics: (CS) representation of information as diagrams, pictures, animation.

Hierarchy: (Math & CS) collection of tree structures; in ER structures each arc is usually a one to many relationship.

Homonym: (ENL) term with two or more different meanings.

Identifier: (ENL) a way by which something can be recognized and referred to. (IS) 1 entity identifier. 2 composite attributes that another is functionally dependent upon.

Image: (Math) value (in the codomain) obtained as a result of a mapping or function, e.g. from 3 by the function squaring the image is 9.
(IS) picture, pictorial representation - e.g. as in 'image processing', screen representation where the intensity of the pixels carries information (if graphical).

Inference: (Math and IS) something inferred (i.e. deduced logically) from the axioms.

Information: (IS) understandable useful relevant communication received at appropriate time; any kind of knowledge about things and concepts in a universe of discourse that is exchangeable between users; it is the meaning that matters, not the representation.

Information base: (IS) a collection of sentences that are consistent with each other and with the conceptual schema, that express the propositions other than the necessary propositions that hold for a universe of discourse.

Information flow: message or information from one area or process to another.

Information flow diagram IFD: (IS) diagram showing flows between areas; may show storage, i.e. show information bases.

Information-process relationship: (IS& CS) association between information type and process type, e.g. what used where.

Information processor: a mechanism that in response to a command executes an action such as retrieval, update or a combination.

Information system IS: means of catering for flows and storage of all relevant information for all EUs; includes CS, information base, information processor.

Information technology (IT): developing and using computing, communications, electronics and related technologies for improving services involving information handling and provision.

Instance: (ENL) an example or occurrence of something
(IS) as ENL | an element of some collection e.g. an occurrence of some named type of something.

Iterative: repeating so as to refine and improve.

Language: agreed way of expressing facts, information, having agreed syntax preferably.

Lexical object = lo: (IS) the lexical string that refers to an actual object.

Lexical object type = lot: (IS) class of such in NIAM.

Local area: functional area, or application area, department, division, section.

Local CDM: CDM for local area.

Logical: (IS) fitting the rules of available software, DBMS; not conceptual; not physical.

Logical database description: (IS) schema, or diagrammatic and descriptive equivalent.

Management-oriented documentation: working paper(s) relating to project reports, present status, policy and organization, costs and benefits, contractual agreements and interviews.

Mandatory retention: (IS) entity or record occurrence must continue to belong to some occurrence of a relationship type.

Many: none, one or several.

Member: (IS) the entity type in a relationship which is not the owner; at the to-many end. (Math) an element belonging to a set.

Membership: (IS) how an entity occurrence participates in a relationship.

Message: flow of information from one actor, usually a user, to another or to or from the information system; a collection of sentences and/or commands.

Meta: appertaining to the description or structure of something; e.g. rule about the structure of the something. Used in terms such as meta-description, meta-language, meta-level.

Model: (ENL) an object representing something else, usually a simpler equivalent preserving the main features.
(IS) mapping of the RW, usually simpler but preserving important relevant features.

Name: (ENL) a word or words by which a person or object is known or referred to.
(IS) same, but usually the names are all different (i.e. unique).

Necessary proposition: proposition asserted to hold always for the universe of discourse, e.g. rule that is always true in the UOD.

Network: nodes and arcs; e.g. entity and relationship types; communication paths; generally more complex than a hierarchy.

Network model: model as network; e.g. EAR, Codasyl; not a hierarchy or tree structure.

Non-lexical object = nolo: (IS) an object in the universe of discourse.

Non-lexical object type: = nolot: (IS) a class of such, named; e.g. an entity type name, in NIAM.

Normalization: (IS) technique for deriving entity types in 3NF, 4NF, 5NF; three main methods: 1 from un-normalized through 1NF, 2NF, 3NF; 2 programmed procedure; 3 via aggregates.

Object: (IS) object in the universe of discourse; entity.

Object class: (IS) class of such; named type, but not necessarily entity type in CDM.

Objective: statement setting forth an intended actual state of affairs, e.g. in behavioural terms.

Occurrence: (ENL) a thing that happened. (IS) an instance of a (named) type of something.

Operation: simple process regarded as atomic.

Optional attribute: (IS) occurrences may or may not exist, e.g. Telephone-no of building.

Optional retention: (IS) entity or record occurrences may belong and cease to belong.

Organization: (ENL& IS) the organization to which the users belong or to which the IS refers | a socio-technical system with some global structure and aims.

Organizational unit: a part of an organization; e.g. company, division, department, section, group.

Owner: (IS) the entity type or entity at the to-one or to-none-or-one end of a relationship type or occurrence.

Performance indicator: a variable whose value shows whether or to what extent a goal or objective has been achieved, e.g. percentage of products available on promised dates.

Phase: (IS) a named collection of development activities; e.g. between decisions.

Phenomenon: (ENL& IS) a thing that appears or is perceived, e.g. something in the RW and perceived.

Physical database description: (IS) storage structure description; i.e. storage schema.

Pilot: the live running of a small part of a system, e.g. as a trial before the rest goes live. It uses data obtained from the actual operations of a business to effect a realistic system for testing by closely simulating the real-world environment.

Population: how many members of a class or set.

Postcondition: (IS& CS) state that must happen at the time that a process finishes.

Precision: (Math) measure of relative accuracy, e.g. maximum percentage error, e.g. rounded to a certain number of significant figures.

Precondition: (IS& CS) state that must happen before/at the time that a process can start.

Primitive: 1 first cut version; crude first attempt at; skeleton version. 2 atomic concept; e.g. entity, entity property, property value, relationship from which other concepts are built.

Privacy: moral right of no unauthorized misuse of information or resources.

Process: sequence of actions, operations, changes; e.g. using and creating data.

Process type: named class of similar processes.

Process analysis: (IS) analysis oriented, e.g. to input, output, processing rules, models of such.

Process dependency: (IS) two processes related by one needing a result from the other.

Process model: (IS) conceptual process model; or logical process model.

Processor: the object that acts in doing a process - may be human or machine.

Program: (CS) coding of how to perform a logical process or class of such.

Project steering committee: a committee specially formed to guide the development of a project. This group is comprised of all senior management who have an interest in a specific project.

Property: named characteristic of an entity.

Proposition: a conceivable state of affairs concerning entities about which it is possible to assert or deny that such a state of affairs holds for those entities. A proposition may be true or false.

Prototype: draft version of implemented system (or part of it) to help development.

Query Language QL: easy method of coding queries, enquiries, retrievals.

Range: (Math) The collection of valid or allowable values.

Real World (=RW): (IS) The part of the physical world that is relevant and perceived.

Relation: (ENL) two or more objects (e.g. people) associated (e.g. in same family.
(Math) subset of a Cartesian product of two sets; i.e. the set of pairs that are associated, where the first of each pair is from one set and the second of each pair is from the second set. (IS) set of n-tuples with values from corresponding domains.

Relationship occurrence: (IS) an association between entities.

Relationship type: (IS) a class of such; named in one or both directions; having degree and existence conditions.

Retention: (IS) rule about allowable changes to currently occurring relationship occurrences.

Retention class: (IS) class or rule for all occurrences of a particular relationship type.

Retrieve: find relevant currently stored data.

Role: the meaning of the part played by, e.g. an attribute value.

Rule: see necessary proposition.

RW: see real world.

Schema: (IS) logical data model, processable by DBMS.

Security: mechanisms for enforcing desired privacy | ...

Sentence: the expression of a proposition as terms and predicates in a language; a linguistic object.

Set: (Math) a collection of elements or members.

Sign: (IS& ENL) a character or symbol or combinations of such, e.g. words, sentences, signals, message | (widened to) equivalent of such, e.g. gesture, facial expression, observable feature (e.g. medically observable).

Simulation: is a mathematical representation of problems showing physical situations as a means of solving the problems created by the factors of the physical processes.

Statement: (Math and logic) something that can be evaluated to be found either true or false. (Programming) an executable small part of a program.

Storage schema SS: physical storage structure description, processable by DBMS.

Strategic planning: means the examination of the current and future needs of an organization.

Subentity type: (IS) subclass of an entity type, e.g. 'clerical staff' within 'staff'.

Subschema: (IS) view of part of a schema relevant for an application; occurrences derivable by DBMS.

Symbol: (IS) the characters or elements of an agreed alphabet, e.g. letters, digits, punctuation marks, layout characters that can occur.

Synonym: (ENL) different term for the same meaning an another, e.g. 'writer' is synonym for 'author'.

System: formed from parts and considered as a collective whole.

System data model: represents a subset of the types of data described by the system group data model; it describes information which is of interest to a system development project team. It is first formulated in summary draft, as a subset of the corporate of system group model. Later, during systems design it becomes more detailed and refined in order that it is able to support the business function data models.

System event: is typically something that will cause a processing, as opposed to a business, function to act upon data on time. For example, the production of a 'report request record' by an online program can be used to trigger production of a report.

System group: a group of related systems that share a significant amount of stored data or transfer significant amounts of data among themselves. Two examples are a company's financial systems and its manufacturing systems.

Systems analysis: (IS) analysis oriented to the computerized aspects and parts therein, e.g. into programs.

Task: piece of work; smaller than or equal to a subphase.

Technical design: Translation of a user-expressed design into a design that will be machine efficient, easy to implement and effective.

Term: linguistic object that refers to an entity.

Third normal form: (IS) entity type or relation structured so every attribute (or collection of such) that any other is functionally dependent on is a candidate identifier.

To many: (IS) occurrences are associated to none, one or several.

To one: (IS) either associated to one; or associated to none or one.

Transaction: piece of business performed, logical unit of equivalent input, processing and results.

Transition: (GST) a change of state from one state to another, usually considered to happen instantaneously.

Tree: (Math) structure starting from a root node and with branching at any node till leaf nodes reached, where no branches meet again. (IS) similar structure of one-to-many relationships going away from root, with entities at the nodes.

Trigger: (ENL) to cause or initiate action. (IS) an event 'triggers' a process, e.g. receipt of a message such as a command or query (= an event) triggers starting the process of finding the answer.

Tuning: (IS) fine adjustment of performance; e.g. by altering storage schema details.

Tuple: (IS) row of relation; n-tuple; in each tuple of a relation the order of the columns is the same.

Type: a recognized class of similar things; usually given a name.

Unique: (IS) each occurrence has a different value.

Universe of discourse UOD: (IS) all those entities that have been, are or ever might be.

Update: (IS) create, modify or delete stored data; may also involve retrieval.

User: synonym for end-user.

User design: translation of a set of user-defined requirements into a design which can be evaluated and examined by the users for whom it is destined.

Value: (Math) an instance from the range that a variable can take. (IS) an instance from the range that an attribute or data item can take.

View: (IS) structure as made available from one process to another, e.g. from DBMS to an application program or to query language for an end-user.

Work plan: a list of all work steps to be performed, the skills required, the estimated effort and key completion dates. Synonymous with installation schedule.

Work station: a physical location where a collection of tasks or procedures are performed by a cohesive group of personnel who share a common view of certain types of information or business functions.

APPENDIX 3

BIBLIOGRAPHY

I think that each reference cited has been looked at by at least one of the authors.

ABBO81: J. Abbott, C. Campbell, A.H. Jones & F.F. Land. BCS Business Information Systems Specialist Group. New Approaches to Systems Analysis and Design. *Information Technology for the Eighties*. Edited R.D. Pavslow (1981).

ANON78: Anon. Data Dictionary Systems. *EDP Analyser* (January 1978).

ANON79: Anon. Production of Better Software. *EDP Analyser* (February 1979).

ANON79: Anon. What Information Do Managers Need? *EDP Analyser* (June 1979).

ANON82: Anon. Special Report. *Computer World* (26 April 1982). Software Design.

ASAN76: Asany & Adomaricz. Data Base Systems. *IBM Systems Journal* (1976) No.3. Data Handling Techniques.

AVIS88a: D.E. Avison & G. Fitzgerald. *Information System Development Methodologies, Techniques and Tools*. Blackwell (1988) pp320. ISBN 0 632 01644 2 (cloth) & 01645 0 (pbk).

AVIS88b: D.E. Avison, G. Fitzgerald & A.T. Wood-Harper. Information Systems Development: A Tool Kit is not Enough. *Computer J*. 31 4 (1988) p379-380.

AWAD88: Elias M. Awad. *Management Information Systems Concepts, Structure and Applications*. Benjamin/Cummings, Ca, USA (1988). ISBN 0-8053-5110-8.

BACH77: C. Bachman. Why Restrict the Modelling Capabilities of CODASYL Data Structure Sets? *Proceedings of National AFIPS Conference* (1977).

BARR79: O. Barros, V. Perez & A. Holgado. Structured logical design of information systems: a methodology, documentation and experience. *Information Systems* 4 1 (1979) pp13-21. ISSN 0306-4379

BEHL86: Robert Behling. *Computers and Information Processing*. Kent, Boston, Mass. USA (1986).

BRIG86: Richard W. Brightman & J.M. Dimsdale. *Using Computers in an Information Age* Delmar, Albany NY (1986). ISBN 0-8273-2372-7.

BRIT62: British Standard 3527: 1962. *Glossary of Terms used in Automatic Data Processing*. British Standard Institution (1962).

BURN86: D. C. Burnstine. *BIAIT: An Emerging Management Engineering Discipline*. BIAIT International (1986). [BIAIT stands for Business Information Analysis and Integration Technique.]

BUSH45: Vannevar Bush. As we may think. *Atlantic Monthly* (July 1945). Reprinted in *Computer Bulletin* Vol 4 Pt 1 (Mar 1988) pp35-40.

CHEN76: P.P.S. Chen. The Entity Relationship Model - Toward a Unified View of Data. *ACM Transactions on DB Systems* Vol. 1. No. 1 (1976).

CHEN80: Chen, P.P. (Ed.) Entity relationship approach to systems analysis and design. *Proceedings International Conference on entity relationship approach to systems analysis and design 1979*. Los Angeles. North Holland (1980).

CHEN83: P.P. Chen (Ed.) Entity relationship approach to information modelling and analysis. *Proceedings 2nd International Conference on entity-relationship approach 1981*. Washington. North Holland (1983).

CLAR86: Raymond T. Clarke & C.A. Prins. *Contemporary Systems Analysis and Design*. Wadsworth, Belmont, Ca, USA (1986). ISBN 0-534-04233-3.

CLAR88: Stephen Clarke. The Increasing Importance of Formal Methods. *Computer Bulletin*. Vol 4 Pt 1 (Mar 1988) pp22-23, 26.

CODD70: E. Codd. A Relational Model of Data for Large Stored Data Banks. *ACM* Vol 13 No.6 (1970).

COOK83: M.J. Cookson. Taxonomic Studies on current approaches to Systems analysis. *Computer J.* Vol 25 No 3 (1983) pp283-284.

COUG82: *Advanced System Development/Feasibility Techniques*. Edited by J. D. Cougar, M. A. Coulter & R. W. Knapp. Wiley (1982).

CRIS 1 and CRIS 2: see OLLE82 and OLLE83.

DATE81: C.J. Date. *An Introduction to Data Base Systems*. Addison Wesley (1981, 1977, 1975). ISBN 0-201-14471-9, 0-201-14456-5.

DDSWP82: British Computer Society DDSWP *Data Dictionary Systems Working Party Journal of Development*. K.H. Meyer, C.C. Morse (Eds.) (1982).

DERR85: Richard L. Derr. The concept of information in ordinary discourse. *Information Processing and Management* 21 6 (1985) pp489-499. [5 necessary features of info: info must be a representation; the representation be abstract; be meaningful; consists of determinations that have been made; the determination have been made of certain objects.]

DUYN82: J.Van Duyn. *Developing a Data Dictionary System.* Prentice Hall (1982). ISBN 0-13-204289-4.

ELLI79: H.C. Ellis. The Entity Use Model. *IFIP* (April 1979).

FITZ85: G. Fitzgerald, N. Stokes & J.R.G. Wood. Feature Analysis of Comtemporary Information Systems Methodologies. *Computer J.* 28 3 (1985) p223-230.

GRIE82: J.J. van Griethuysen (Ed.). ISO TC97/SC5/WG3, *Concepts and Terminology for the Conceptual Schema and the Information Base.* (1982).

GRIF78: S.N. Griffiths. Design Methodologies - A Comparison. In *Pergamon Infotech State Of The Art Reports* Vol 2 No. 4 (1978).

GUEZ80: J-C. Guez. Database Design Experience with IMS. In *PergamonInfotech State-of-the-Art Report on Database* (1980).

HEID82: Heidrick & Struggles.*Information Technology: The Management of Change in the United Kingdom in 1982.* 25-28 Old Burlington St. London W1X 2BD.

IBM75: Business Systems Planning. IBM (1975). [Reprinted in Coug82.] [Our Chapter 3 BSP is *not* based on IBM's BSP.]

INMO81: W. Inmon. *Effective Data Base Design.* Prentice Hall (1981). ISBN 0-13-241489-9.

INMO82: W. Inmon & Friedman. *Design Review Methodology.* Prentice Hall (1982). ISBN 0-13-201392-4.

KENT78: William Kent. *Data and Reality.* North-Holland.04-44-85187-9.

KRAS81: Peter Krass & Hesh Wienor. The DBMS Market is Booming: Survey of 54 DBMS. *Datamation* (September 1981).

LOMA77: J.D. Lomax. *Data Dictionary Systems.* NCC Publications (1977) ISBN 0-85012-191-4.

LUCA86: Henry C. Lucas. *Introduction to Computers and Information Systems.* Macmillan, Canada (1986). ISBN 0-02-372210-X.

MADD59: R.N. Maddison. *Commercial Applications of Computers.* Thesis. Oxford (1959).

MADD78: Richard N. Maddison (Ed). *Data Analysis for Information System Design.* British Computer Society Conference Proceedings 29 June 1978 (out of print 1988).

MADD84: R.N. Maddison & A.J. Gawronski. A Data Dictionary for Learning Data Analysis. (DADICS). In *Computer Journal* Vol 28 No.3 (July 1985) pp270-281.

MADD85: R.N. Maddison. *Information System Methodologies.* Pergamon Infotech State-of-the-Art Report *The Corporate Database* 13 3 (May 1985).

MART80: J. Martin. *Strategic Data Planning Methodologies.* Savant, Carnforth, Lancashire, UK. (1908). [Describes IBM's Business Strategic Planning, which is *not* the same as our BSP in our Chapter 3. See also IBM70.]

MAYN81: Alan Mayne. *Database Management Systems: A Technical Review.* NCC Publications (1981) ISBN 0-85012-323-2.

McCR82: D.D. McCracken & M.A. Jackson.Life Cycle Concept Considered Harmful. *Software Engineering Notes* Vol 7 No. 2 (April 1982).

MING88: J. Mingers. Comparing Conceptual Models and Data Flow Diagrams. *Computer J.* Vol. 31, No. 4 (August 1988) pp376-8.

MOSE87: Jorge Moser & R. Christoph. Management Expert Systems (MES): a framework for development and implementation. *Information Processing & Management* 23 1 (1987) pp17-23.

MUMF83: E. Mumford. *Designing Human Systems.* Manchester Business School (1983).

MUMF84: Enid Mumford. Participative Systems Design. [Short note].*Computer J.* 27 3 (1984) p283.

NIJS77: G.M. Nijssen (Ed.). Architecture and Models in Data Base Management Systems. *Proceedings of the IFIP Working Conference on Modelling in Data Base Management Systems.* North Holland (1977) ISBN 0-7204-0758-3.

NISJ76: G.M. Nijssen. A Gross Architecture for the Next Generation Database Management System. Modelling in Database Management Systems. *Proc. IFIP Working Conference.* North Holland Pub. Co. Amsterdam (1976).

NISS83: H.-E. Nissen. Subject matter separability in Information System Design Methods. In CRIS2 pp207.

OLLE78: T.William Olle. *The CODASYL Approach to Data Base Management.* John Wiley & Sons. ISBN 0-471-99579-7, reprinted with corrections 1980.

185

OLLE82: T.W. Olle, H.G. Sol & A.A. Verrijn-Stuart (Eds.). Information Systems Design Methodologies: A Comparative Review. *Proceedings of the IFIP TC 8 Working Conference on Comparative Review of Information Systems Design Methodologies*, Noordwijkerhout, The Netherlands, 10-14 May 1982. North Holland, Amsterdam, (1982). We call this CRIS1.

OLLE83: T.W. Olle, J.G. Sol, & C.J. Tully (Eds.). Information Systems Design Methodologies: A Feature analysis. *Proceedings of the IFIP WG8.1 Working Conference on Feature Analysis of Information Systems Design Methodologies*, York, UK, 5-7 July, 1983. North Holland (1983). We call this CRIS2.

OLLE88: T. William Olle, Jacques Hagelstein, Ian G. Macdonald, Collette Rolland, Henke G. Sol, Frans J.M. Van Assche & Alexander A. Verrijn-Stuart. *Information System Methodologies - A Framework For Understanding.* Report prepared by CRIS Task Group of IFIP Working Group 8.1 (Design and Evaluation of ISs).

OU M352: M352 *Computer-based Information Systems.* The Open University Press. (1980)ISBN 0 335 14000 9 to 0 335 14005 X; also 4 Activity Booklets and 4 Study Guides.

OU PM681: PM681 *Data Analysis For Information System Design.* The Open University Press. (1983) ISBN 0 335 10315 4; also Activity Book, Study Guide, STC Case Study ISBN 0 335 14005 X.

ROBI81: Hugh Robinson. *Database Analysis and Design.* Chartwell-Bratt (1981). ISBN 0-86238-018-9, 91-44-18781-5.

ROSE82: C.J. Rosenquist. Entity Life Cycle Models and their Applicability to Information Systems Development Life Cycles: A Framework for Information Systems Design and Implementation. *Computer J.* 25 3 (1982) pp307.

ROUS86: William B. Rouse. On the value of information in system design: a framework for understanding and aiding designers. *Information Processing and Management* 22 3 (1986). pp217-228.

RUDK79: Ralph I. Rudkin & Kenneth D. Shere. Structured Decomposition Diagram: A New Technique for Systems Analysis. *Datamation* (October 1979). [Functional Systems Analysis.]

SAVA85: Nigel Savage & C. Edwards. *A Guide to the Data Protection Act.* Financial Training, London (1985). 2nd. Ed. ISBN 0-906322-92-8.

SENK73: H. Senko et al. Data Structures and Accessing in Database Systems. *IBM Systems Journal* Vol 12 No. 1 (1973).

SWAR82: W. Swartout & R. Balzen. On the Inevitable Intertwining of Specification and Implementation. *Communications of the ACM* 25 7 (July 1982).

TAGG80. Roger M. Tagg. *Data Design in Practice.* Pergamon Infotech State-of-the-Art Report on Database (1980).

V-ST87: A. Verrijn-Stuart. Themes and Trends in ISs: TC8 1975-1985. *Computer J.* Vol 30 No 2 (Apr 1987) pp97-109. See also its refs, including a list of TC8 publications.

VETT81: M. Vetter & R.N. Maddison. *Database Design Methodology.* Prentice-Hall (1981) ISBN 0-13-196535-2.

WELD81: Jay-Louise Weldon.*Data Base Administration.*Plenum Press. ISBN 0-3096-40595-4.

WIND80: A.T. Windsor. *Using the ICL Data Dictionary: Proceedings of the User Group.* Shiva Publishing Ltd (1980).

WOOD82: A.T. Wood-Harper & G. Fitzgerald. A taxonomy of Current Approaches to Systems Analysis. *Computer J.* Vol 25 No 1 (Feb 1982) 12-16.

References for particular methodologies

For ACM/PCM:

BROD80: M.L. Brodie. *Data Quality in Information Systems Information and Management* 3 (1980) pp245-258.

BROD80: M.L. Brodie. The Application of Data Types to Database Semantic Integrity. *Information Systems.* Vol. 5, 4 (1980) pp287-296.

BROD81: M. Brodie. On Modelling Behavioural Semantics of Databases. *Proceedings: 1981 International Conference on very large Databases*, Cannes, France, September 1981.

BROD81: M.L. Brodie. Association: A Database Abstraction for Semantic Modelling. *Proceedings: 2nd International Entity-Relationship Conference*, Washington, D.C. (October 1981). In CHEN83.

BROD81: M.L. Brodie. Data Abstraction for Designing Database-Intensive Applications. In Brodie, M.L. & Zilles, S.N. (Eds.) *Proceedings: Workshop on Data Abstraction, Databases and Conceptual Modelling.* SIGPLAN Notices 16, 1 (1981) pp101-103.

BROD82: M.L. Brodie & E. Silva. Active and Passive Component Modelling, *CRIS1 proceedings* pp41-91.

RIDJ82: D. Ridjanovic & M.L. Brodie. *Semantic Data Model-Driven Design, Specification and Verification of Interactive Database Transactions* (Apr1982) pp215.

SMIT77: J.M. Smith & D.C.P. Smith. Database Abstraction: Aggregation and generalization. *ACM Transactions On Database Systems* 2 2 (June 1977) pp105-133.

For DDSS:

DAVE78: R.A. Davenport. Data analysis for data base design. *Australian Computer J.* 10 (1978) pp122-137.

MACD82: I.G. MacDonald & I.R. Palmer. System Development in a Shared Data Environment, the DDSS Methodology. CRIS1 pp237-283.

PALM78: I.R. Palmer. Practicalities in applying a formal methodology to data analysis. In *Data Analysis For Information System Design: Conference papers* 29 June 1978. Maddison, R.N. (Ed.) (1978).

ROCK81: R. Rock-Evans.Data Analysis. *Computer Weekly* and book, IPC Business Press (1981). ISBN 0-617-00372-6.

SHAV81: M.J.R. Shave. Entities, functions and binary relations: steps to a conceptual schema. *Computer J.* 24 (1981) pp42-47.

For ISAC:

ANON79: EDP 79: The Analysis of User Needs. *EDP Analyser* 17 1 (Jan 1979).

DAVI82: G.B. Davis. Strategies for information requirements determination. *IBM Systems J.* 21 1 (1982) pp18-19.

HANI86: Michael Z. Hanani & P. Shoval. A combined methodology for information systems analysis and design based on ISAC and NIAM. *Information Systems* 11 3 (1986) pp245-253. [The business and information analysis of ISAC is combined with the conceptual process of NIAM.]

LUND75: M. Lundeburg. Four important problems in analysis and design of information systems. *Systemeering 75* (Eds. M. Lundeburg & J. Bubenko Jnr). Published by Studentlitteratur (1975) pp38-73. ISBN 9144114311.

LUND79: Ditto: II: Problem and data oriented methodology. *Information Systems* Vol. 4 2 (1979) pp93-118. Oxford: Pergamon Press.

LUND79: M. Lundeburg, G. Goldkuhl & A. Nilssen. A systematic approach to information systems development - I: Introduction. *Information Systems* Vol. 4 1 (1979) pp1-12.

LUND81: M. Lundeburg, G. Goldkuhl, & A. Nilssen. *Information systems development - a systematic approach.* Prentice-Hall (1981) ISBN 0-13-464677-0.

LUND82. M. Lundeburg. The ISAC Approach to Specification of Information Systems and its Application to the Organization of an IFIP Working Conference. CRIS1 pp173-234.

For JSD:

IFIP Problem. Ref 'APCBE-1'. MJSL. (1982 or 1983) pp190-215.Michael Jackson. *System Development.* Prentice-Hall (1983) ISBN 0-13-880328-5.

JSD *A Manager's Guide to the System Development Method.* Michael Jackson Systems Limited (Undated, about 1982) pp10.

JSD Technical Summary. *MJSL* ('1982-1983') pp17.

For LBMS, SSADM and LSDM:

CUTT87: Geoff Cutts. *Structured Systems Analysis and Design Methodology.* Paradigm. (1987) 425pp. Also ISBN 0 948825 86 3 paperback (1988).

HALL81: J. Hall. *System Development Methodology. LBMS* (March 1981).

LBMS87: *Training for ISs development.* [Brochure] (1987). pp34.

For NIAM:

VERH82: G.M.A. Verheijen & J. Van Bekkum. NIAM: An Information Analysis Method. CRIS1 pp537-589.

For SASD:

DEMA78: T. De Marco. *Structured analysis and system specification.* Yourdon Press (1978) ISBN 0-917072-07-3.

For STRADIS SDM:

GANE79: Chris Gane & Trish Sarson. *Structured Systems Analysis: Tools and Techniques.* Prentice-Hall (1979). ISBN 0-13-854547-2.

MCAUTO *STRADIS System Development Methodology Product Description.* (Undated, about 1982) pp20.

PAGE82: M. Page-Jones. *Practical guide to structured systems design.* Yourdon Press (1982) ISBN 0-917072-17-0.

STEV74: W.P. Stevens, G.J. Myers & L.L. Constantine. Structured Design. *IBM System Journal* 13 2 (1974) pp115-139.

YOUR75: Edward N. Yourdon. *Techniques of Program Structure and Design*, Prentice Hall ISBN 0-13-901702-X.

YOUR78: Yourdon, E.N. & Constantine, L.L. *Structured Design*. Yourdon Press and Prentice-Hall (1978) ISBN 0-13-854471-9. (1979) ISBN 0-13-854547-2.

YOUR79: Edward N. Yourdon. *Structural Design: Fundamentals of a discipline of computer program and systems design*. Prentice Hall ISBN 01-13-854471-9.

YOUR81: Edward N. Yourdon (Ed).*Classics in Software Engineering*. Yourdon Press. ISBN 0-917072-14-6.

YOUR82: Edward N. Yourdon. *Managing the System Life-cycle: a software development methodology overview*. Yourdon Press. ISBN 0-917072-26-X.

YOUR82: Edward N. Yourdon. *Writings of the Revolution: selected readings on software engineering*. Yourdon Press. 0-917072-25-1.

For SYSDOC:

ASCH82: F. Aschim & B.M. Mostue. IFIP WG 8.1 Case Solved using Sysdoc and Systemator. CRIS1 pp15-40.

Contacts

BIS Applied Systems. 20 Worple Road, London SW19. 01 633 0866. Also 20 Upper Ground, London SE1 9PN.

LBMS Learmonth & Burchett Management Systems PLC. Evelyn House, 62 Oxford Street, London W1N 9LF. 01 636 4213.

SSADM was jointly developed by LBMS and the CCTA. AUTO-MATE PLUS is a semi-automated tool for SSADM and LSDM and for prototyping, DBMS syntax generation and program code generation.

SYSLAB: University of Stockholm, S-10691 Stockholm, Sweden. Tel + 46 16 20 20.

APPENDIX 4

PRODUCTS AND TASKS

The following lists all products, prerequisites, reports, working papers, and deliverables in roughly the order that they appear in the body of the book. You should remember that a specification, report or plan may be produced in a computer-held form, i.e. it need not be a paper document. The format is as in the index, Appendix 5. In some cases the wording here and in the Appendix 5 Index is shorter than in the main body of the book.

BSP state of the organization in its competitive environment, P, 3.8, 4.6
BSP state key factors for success, P, 3.8, 4.6
BSP statement on existing ISs, P, 3.8, 4.6
BSP corporate outline policy statement on ISs strategy, P, 3.8, 4.6
BSP corporate statement on new ISs and improvements, P, 3.8, 4.6
BSP recommendations, P, 3.8, 4.6
BSP formal presentation, P, 3.8
BSP records of interviews and briefings, P, 3.8
BSP progress and outcome report, P, 3.8
BSP conclusions, P, 3.8
ISSP analysis of the current position, P, 4.8
ISSP profile of the existing ISs, P, 4.8
ISSP data review, P, 4.8
ISSP systems audit, P, 4.8
ISSP statement of ISs objectives, P, 4.8
ISSP list of ISs and objectives, P, 4.8
ISSP technology review, P, 4.8
ISSP likely impact of information technology developments, P, 4.8
ISSP defined alternative strategies, P, 4.8
ISSP defined selection criteria, P, 4.8
ISSP evaluated alternative strategies, P, 4.8
ISSP selected strategy, P, 4.8
ISSP defined migration plan, P, 4.8
ISSP defined component IS, P, 4.8
ISSP TOR for each IS, P, 4.8
ISD plans, P, 4.8
ISSP statement of IS priorities, P, 4.8, 5.6
ISSP impact of IS on organizational structure and management, P, 4.8
ISSP hardware and software acquisition policy, P, 4.8
Technology to be used = equipment acquisition policy, P, 4.8, 5.6

ISSP skills acquisition policy, P, 4.8
ISSP statement of the plans for global data analysis, P, 4.8
ISSP policy on IS standards, P, 4.8
ISSP policy on DA, P, 4.8
ISSP policy on IS quality control, P, 4.8
ISSP policy on IS auditing, P, 4.8
ISSP retrospective report on costs and benefits of existing ISs, P, 4.8
New systems and improvements, P, 4.8
Statement of guidelines on equipment technology communications, P, 4.8, 5.6
More detailed statement of IS objectives, P, (4.8), 5.8
More detailed statement of IS functions, P, 5.8
IS introduction plan, P, 5.8
IS modification plan, P, 5.8
IS cost and benefit analysis report, P, 5.8
Education and training policy and plans for this IS, P, 5.8
Global data analysis report, P, 5.8
TOR for FS, P, 7.6
FS report, P, 5.8, 8.6
Resources for analysis project, P, 8.6
Project steering committee established, P, 8.6
Signed TOR for analysis, P, 8.6
Development time-scales for analysis and subsequent phases, P, 8.6
Analysis progress and exception report, P, 8.8
Analysis functional specifications, P, 8.8
Analysis function charts, P, 8.8, 10.6
Analysis conceptual data models, P, 8.8
Analysis information flow diagrams, P, 8.8
Analysis other data-to-function mapping models, P, 8.8
Analysis business function model, P, 8.8
Analysis requirements report, P, 8.8
Specification of user requirements by functions to be supported, P, 9.6
Global design policy, P, 9.6
Policy guidelines on the resources available, P, 9.6, 9.9
UD specification, P, 9.8, 10.6
UD transition and training plan, P, 9.8, 10.6
Final business data model, P, 10.6
Hardware and software decisions, P, 10.6
Application architecture report, P, 10.6
Application development plan, P, 10.6
Data storage and retrieval policy, P, 10.6
Development environment policy, P, 10.6
TD specification, P, 10.8
TD revised development plan, P, 10.8

TD revisions to TD prerequisites, P, 10.8
TD operating procedures and instructions, P, 10.8.

The following lists all tasks and activities in roughly their order of appearance in the main body of the book:

Define the state of the organization in its competitive environment, T, 3.7
Deduce key factors for success, T, 3.7
Define the profile of existing ISs, T, 3.7
Define the top management objectives for existing ISs, T, 3.7
Define gap between performance and expectations of existing ISs, T, 3.7
Identify relevant issues and alternatives, T, 3.7
Get top management agreement on priorities of requirements, T, 3.7
Write end-of-BSP report, T, 3.7
Plan set up of steering party for strategic planning reviews, T, 3.7
Design and prepare visual aids, T, 3.7
Do end-of-BSP presentation, T, 3.7
Analyse the current position, T, 4.7
Perform data review, T, 4.7
Perform ISs audit, T, 4.7
Define IS objectives, T, 4.7
Perform technology review, T, 4.7
Develop alternative strategies, T, 4.7, 7.7
Define selection criteria, T, 4.7
Evaluate alternative strategies, T, 4.7, 7.7
Select strategy, T, 4.7
Define migration plan, T, 4.7
Define component IS, T, 4.7
Define overall IS standards, T, 4.7
Define hardware and software acquisition policies, T, 4.7
Define skills acquisition policy, T, 4.7
Define development methods policy, T, 4.7
Define t and t policy, T, 4.7
Define DA and process administration policy, T, 4.7
Define design standards, T, 4.7
Define quality control policy, T, 4.7
Define audit procedures policy, T, 4.7
Review ISSP, T, 4.7
Develop the BSP in more detail for ISSP, T, 4.7
Determine the priorities of the ISs, T, 4.7
Establish organizational functional equipment acquisition policy, T, 4.7
Establish organizations IS skills acquisition policy, T, 4.7
Form policy for development methodologies, T, 4.7
Form policy for development hardware software t and t, T, 4.7

Develop ISs standards, T, 4.7
Develop DA policy, T, 4.7
Develop IS quality control policy, T, 4.7
Develop IS audit procedures policy, T, 4.7
Plan the global data analysis, T, 4.7
Evaluate use of IT developments, T, 4.7
Evaluate effects of IT developments, T, 4.7
Plan the reviewing of ISs, T, 4.7
Develop profiles of existing ISs, T, 4.7
Produce statement of the functions and objectives of the IS, T, 5.7
Assess the impact of this IS on the business functions, T, 5.7
Plan this IS's introduction into the EU environment, T, 5.7
Plan EU education and training for this IS, T, 5.7
Plan the management of the initial use of this IS, T, 5.7
Plan the flexibility of this IS, T, 5.7
Plan the mature use of this IS, T, 5.7
Plan the equipment for this IS, T, 5.7
Plan acquisition and installation for this IS, T, 5.7
Plan education and training of development staff for this IS, T, 5.7
Plan this IS project team, T, 5.7
Manage the development task, T, 6.2
Decompose complex tasks into smaller ones, T, 6.3
Analyse the project into actions to be done, T, 6.2, 6.4
Estimate the work content of each action, T, 6.2, 6.4
Plan the work, T, 6.2
Allocate resources, T, 6.2
Control performance, T, 6.2
Report progress, T, 6.2
Control change, T, 6.2
Define start and finish points of each activity, T, 6.3
Prescribe the work-content duration for each activity, T, 6.3
Prescribe observable end-product for each activity, T, 6.3, 6.6
Create hierarchy of phases or stages tasks activities, T, 6.3
Match required jobs to resources available, T, 6.5
Assess progress, T, 6.6
Allocate work in amounts achievable in set periods, T, 6.6
Allocate authority and responsibility for each action, T, 6.8
Allocate adequate staff to the leader, T, 6.8
Ensure a suitable environment for staff to do work, T, 6.8
Draw staff from appropriate experience, T, 6.8
Ensure appropriate open communication among staff, T, 6.8
Ensure plans exist before during and after construction, T, 6.8
Plan the controls on each project and action, T, 6.8
Ensure progress reports are provided, T, 6.8

Ensure feasibility of continuance and completion of project, T, 6.8
State objectives of project phase task activity, T, 6.8
Restate modified objectives of project by agreement, T, 6.8
Make financial justification of project, T, 6.8
Prepare successful documentation of project, T, 6.8
Arrange independent reviews, T, 6.8
Examine for prejudice and preference, T, 6.8
Ensure that project TOR and objectives are clearly understood, T, 6.9
Ensure that manager has skills and access to resources, T, 6.9
Ensure adequate procedures to analyse estimate plan and control, T, 6.9
Ensure arrangements for user participation, T, 6.9
Ensure effective management control, T, 6.9
Specify the area of FS, T, 7.7
Define alternatives, T, 4.7, 7.7
Define criteria for selection, T, 7.7
Evaluate alternatives and strategies, T, 4.7, 7.7
Evaluate assumptions, T, 7.7
Select recommendations, T, 7.7
Document the investigation and its conclusions, T, 7.7
Approve solution recommended, T, 7.7
Update TOR, T, 7.7
Document the chosen solution and work plan, T, 7.7
Do data analysis, T, 8.7
Do functional analysis, T, 8.7
Do activity analysis, T, 8.7
Do event analysis, T, 8.7
Do requirements analysis, T, 8.7
Do analysis of existing systems, T, 8.7
Do completeness checking, T, 8.7
Produce analysis progress and exception report, T, 8.7
Produce functional specifications, T, 8.7
Produce function charts, T, 8.7
Produce conceptual data models, T, 8.7
Produce information flow diagrams, T, 8.7
Produce other data-to-function mapping models, T, 8.7
Produce business function model report, T, 8.7
Produce requirements report, T, 8.7
Decide the best facility to support each function, T, 9.7
Design the computer procedures, T, 9.7
Design the non-computer procedures, T, 9.7
Code implement and test a prototype, T, 9.7
Design and specify the input forms reports and screen layouts, T, 9.7
Finish the global data model, T, 9.7
Estimate response times availability performance, T, 9.7

Review the design to ensure consistency with objectives, T, 9.7
Evaluate the costs and benefits, T, 9.7
Produce transition and training plan, T, 9.7
Produce user-design specification, T, 9.7
Produce reference documentation, T, 9.7
Produce material required for training, T, 9.7
Schedule data conversion, T, 9.7
Schedule changeover, T, 9.7
Produce UD progress and exception report, T, 9.7
Specify detailed hardware and software configuration, T, 10.7
Do logical and physical data design, T, 10.7
Do program design, T, 10.7
Do technical transition design, T, 10.7
Do operational design, T, 10.7
Do sizing, T, 10.7
Evaluate technical design, T, 10.7
Produce TD progress and exception report, T, 10.7

APPENDIX 5

INDEX

Entries refer to the chapter and section, not the page.

G means a term in our glossary, Appendix 2.

P means a product, report, deliverable or prerequisite, as in Appendix 4. Such entries usually give just the section for the product list, e.g. c.8 where c is the chapter. The corresponding description will be in section c.10. The corresponding phase objectives should be regarded as including to produce such product if appropriate for the organization development, whether or not the product is mentioned in section c.4. You are expected to assume that a task or activity to create each product is implied, even if not entered in the index or in Appendix 4, and even if not mentioned in the main body of the book.

R means a reference in our bibliography, Appendix 3. References for particular methodologies and their authors are not necessarily indexed here.

S means see Summary.

T means a development, phase, task, or activity, as in Appendix 4. Entries for tasks usually give just the section of the task list, e.g. c.7 where c is the chapter. Such tasks usually also appear in the corresponding framework diagram in section c.2, and are described in section c.9.

TOR Ap 1 means see Terms of Reference, Appendix 1.